FRANCIS GREENSLADE

HOW I LEARNT TO ACT

On the way to NOT going to drama school

CURRENCY PRESS
The performing arts publisher

First published in 2019
by Currency Press Pty Ltd,
PO Box 2287, Strawberry Hills, NSW, 2012, Australia
enquiries@currency.com.au
www.currency.com.au
Copyright © Francis Greenslade, 2019.

Image copyright: page 6, photo courtesy of Shaun Micallef; page 49, photo copyright © Lisa Tomasetti; page 56, photo copyright © David Wilson; page 65, photo copyright © Eric Algra; page 85, photo courtesy of Media West 7; page 102, photo copyright © Tracey Schramm; page 112, photo copyright © Jeff Busby; page 122, photo copyright © Jeff Busby; page 149 photo copyright © Nikki Hamilton-Cornwall; page 154, photo copyright © Jodie Hutchinson; page 161, photo copyright © Jeff Busby; page 170, photo copyright © Nikki Hamilton-Cornwall.

Copying for Educational Purposes: The Australian Copyright Act 1968 allows a maximum of one chapter or 10% of this book, whichever is the greater, to be copied by any educational institution for its educational purposes provided that the educational institution (or the body that administers it) has given a remuneration notice to Copyright Agency (CA) under the Act. For details of the CA licence for educational institutions, please contact CA: 11/66 Goulburn Street, Sydney, NSW, 2000; tel: within Australia 1800 066 844 toll free; outside Australia +61 2 9394 7600; fax: +61 2 9394 7601; email: info@copyright.com.au

Copying for Other Purposes: Except as permitted under the Act, for example a fair dealing for the purposes of study, research, criticism or review, no part of this book may be reproduced, stored in a retrieval system, or transmitted in any form or by any means without prior written permission. All enquiries should be made to the publisher at the above address.

Cover design Lisa White for Currency Press.
Front cover shows Francis Greenslade in, from left: *Babes in the Wood* (© Jeff Busby); *Mad as Hell* (© ITV); *The Club* (© Eric Algra); *Mad as Hell* (© ITV and Nikki Hamilton-Cornwall). Back cover shows Francis in *The School for Scandal* (© David Wilson).

Currency Press acknowledges the Traditional Owners of the Country on which we live and work. We pay our respects to all Aboriginal and Torres Strait Islander Elders, past and present.

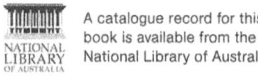
A catalogue record for this book is available from the National Library of Australia

Contents

Contents	iii
Prologue	1
Beginnings	3
Ann	5
My First Acting Lesson	7
The Tax Office	10
I Get a Job	14
The Tempest	17
Alice in Wonderland	22
Kafka's Dick	27
Evensong for Antarctica	29
Wind in the Willows	32
Magpie	35
The Ensemble	41
Prince of Numbskulls	44
Funerals and Circuses, Chutney	48
Marat/Sade	50
School for Scandal	54
Così	61
The Club	63
Accidental Death of an Anarchist	70
Status	71

Moving	77
Blue Heelers	80
Projection	88
Full Frontal	90
Macbeth	94
Blabbermouth	99
Navigating	101
Introducing Gary Petty	103
Man the Balloon	106
Babes in the Wood	110
Sam	114
Take Away	117
The Odyssey	120
Things We Do for Love	123
Winners and Losers	130
The Film Set	133
Screen Acting	135
The Grosses	138
Time and Other Issues	141
Mad as Hell	145
You Got Older	151
The Odd Couple	155
Reviews	164
Teaching	166
Teaching Comedy	174
My Mantra	182
Three Things	183
Acknowledgements	186
Bibliography	187

Prologue

'Hey, you're that actor, aren't you?'

'Well, I am *an* actor, so yes, I suppose so.'

'I knew it! Cool ... Hey, how do you learn your lines?'

If I've heard that once I've heard it – ooh, eleven times? Maybe even twelve. It slightly depresses me. It implies that acting is only about the mental retention of the script. That all I really need to do is memorise a list of words and bang – there I am in front of the camera acting my little heart out. I usually reply that it's not the actual learning of lines that is the difficult part, it's the working out how to say them.

But I do think the question is indicative of a lack of understanding about acting in this country. I'm not sure Australians in general really understand what *acting* really is.

Overseas it's different. In the United Kingdom they seem to revere their actors. They give them honours and peerages. Dame Judy and Sir Ian. Baron Olivier. This is the country that gave birth to William Shakespeare. He spoke English. I'm English. He walked down the same street I'm walking down now. Doesn't it make you proud? And consequently there seems to be a little more understanding about the power of language and a little more respect for those who can manipulate it.

In the United States they had the Method and the Studio, Marlon Brando appearing and tearing up the rule book. Actors with great emotional connectivity talking about their dog dying and bursting into floods of cathartic tears. Meryl and Dustin and Philip Seymour Hoffman and Bryan Cranston and Frances McDormand. All masters of their craft. That performance as What'shisname! Brilliant!

In Australia, we revere actors too. But generally only if they've made it in the States. Russell and Cate are great not because they're technically competent actors or gifted artists, but because they're in big American blockbusters. And we're not much interested in their acting, just how much they're paid and what the film brought in the first week it opened. And perhaps how they learn their lines.

Or maybe I'm overgeneralising wildly.

But at any rate there is something more to it than just memorising words and I hope this book can cast some light on what exactly that is.

This is not by any means a method. There are some really good books around that can take you from go to whoa: *The Intent to Live* by Larry Moss and *Fine on Acting* by Howard Fine are two good places to start; *The Actor and the Target* by Declan Donnellan is a really interesting and slightly different way of looking at acting (and life), and *Dimensions of Acting* by Terence Crawford gives an Australian perspective. I found the latter two, especially, quite fascinating.

And I'm not Laurence Olivier or Judi Dench, I don't have a swag of great roles behind me, I'm not even that well known. I'm a reasonably competent, not unsuccessful actor that's managed to get enough work over his career to ensure that he doesn't have to work in a bottle shop. But I'm never the lead. I was William McInnes' best friend, the stooge that Max Gillies hired to kill the children, the guy that Shaun Micallef threw the fish at.

But then not many actors *are* Laurence Olivier or Judi Dench. Most working actors are like me. We get a guest role here, a nice part in a stage show there, and, if we're lucky, a regular spot in a TV series. We keep working, but no-one knows our name. In fact we keep working *because* no-one knows our name.

So as long as we're clear. No pretensions to greatness. No suggestion that there's any sort of rigorous theory behind this. I've just picked up a craft over 30-odd years of practising it. It won't be everyone's cup of tea. And you will certainly disagree with some of the things I say. I'm not the best driver in the world, but I have been driving my particular vehicle around for about 30 years now, and I understand the mechanism and how to get it to work.

And I hope that at the very least it will demonstrate that there's a little more to the whole shebang than just learning the lines.

Beginnings

My first theatrical performance of any major significance occurred in Mrs Wilson's Grade 2 class at Belair Infant School. We were to put on a circus performance. We would be both the audience and the acts. Everyone got to choose their role. Some children wanted to be acrobats and some were going to be wild animals. Jeremy Atkinson, an irritating boy, claimed ringmaster before anyone else could open their mouths. I didn't mind. There was no question as to what I would be. I would be a clown. Clowns are funny. They make people laugh. How extraordinarily fabulous.

As time went on, and the acrobats practised their tricks and the lions practised their roaring, I began to have some doubts about the wisdom of my choice. And when the day of doing the damn thing actually arrived, I realised that while I wanted to *be* a clown, I had no idea of what to actually *do*. In other words, I didn't have an act. And the thought of going out in front of an audience with nothing prepared was, and still is, completely, utterly and immobilisingly terrifying.

The performance started. I quit. I found a chair at the back of the room and sat there. The teacher and some of the other students gathered round me and tried to cajole me on stage. It was kind of them but unsuccessful. I was not going out into that gaping black maw without an act. I'd get swallowed up and die. No thank you.

The circus went on without me. The animals did tricks. The acrobats acrobatted. The audience roared their approval. And eventually the fear that I was going to miss out made me so desperate that an idea finally presented itself. I took a cowboy hat and hung it round my neck so that it dangled behind me. I went on stage. The audience quietened expectantly. I took a deep breath.

'Where's my hat?'

'Behind you', came the reply.

I turned around to find it wasn't there. And when I turned back to inform the audience that they were wrong, I was rewarded with the biggest laugh I had ever elicited in my short life.

'No it isn't. Where is it?'

Et cetera.

Not original or even clever but it worked. We're talking about a fairly unsophisticated audience, after all. And I can still feel that addictive rush of wild public affirmation.

I continued with the schtick for as long as I thought the audience would buy it and then, flushed with success, I made a low bow and flinging myself back up, slipped and banged my head violently on the floor behind me, probably only saved from real damage by the hat, conveniently in position.

I was helped from the stage and ended up back in the seat I had started from, being tended to and comforted by the same group who had provoked me into the dangerous world of performing in the first place.

And I discovered two things that day. ***How extraordinarily exciting the stage is and also how extremely dangerous.*** Two poles between which I have swung ever since.

Ann

It only took me a decade to recover from the shock of that first performance, but by the time I left school I was fascinated by the theatre. My mother had often taken me to plays when I was younger. Colin George was Artistic Director of the State Theatre Company in Adelaide and he put on the classics: *The Cherry Orchard*, *The School for Scandal*, *Macbeth*. The actors I saw up on stage were the most confident, brave, vulnerable, sexy people I had ever seen. They were superhuman. I knew from bitter experience how dangerous it was up there. I could never do that. It was too scary. But my God, it looked exciting.

By 1989, I had changed my mind. I had been to uni. I had met a student called Shaun Micallef who would go on to become the most brilliant comedian of his generation and a good friend. I had been on stage in revues with Adelaide University Footlights and as a consequence I was getting quite good at putting on a suit, sitting behind a desk and saying 'Come in Mr Edwards' in a funny voice. I could do sketch comedy, or at least I was learning to, but I had absolutely no idea how to act, or how one went about making a career out of it.

Drama school was a possibility. Melbourne's Victorian College of the Arts (VCA) and Sydney's National Institute of Dramatic Arts (NIDA) were the main two. But the idea that I might audition, that I could find a monologue, that I could do it properly, that I could afford the audition fee, that they would accept me, that I could support myself while interstate at drama school – all these were impossible to imagine. It was several bridges too far.

Then I got an agent. I'm not sure how. One minute I was coming off stage after a uni revue and the next minute a woman put a piece of paper with a phone number in my hand and told me to call her tomorrow. Not fair. I know that getting an agent is in many respects the most difficult thing for a would-be actor to do. I know that it's a catch-22 situation: you can't get work without an agent, and you can't get an agent unless you have work to show them. I know all this. But in my case, it happened before I was even conscious that I needed one. Sorry.

A blurry photograph of Shaun Micallef hitting the author with a riding crop. Cheap Mucky Trash, *Adelaide University Footlights. (Photo courtesy of Shaun Micallef)*

At any rate, the redoubtable Ann Peters took me on. She ran a casting business called SA Casting. It is probably closer to the mark to say she *was* casting in South Australia as everything seemed to come through her. And she is still going strong as far as I'm aware.

Ann was scary. I was scared of her. But I liked her greatly as well. She had no hesitation in telling me when she thought my work was bad. Which was often. She put up with my naivety and constant queries about money and work. She advanced me money out of her own purse when I was in difficulties and productions hadn't paid up.

And she gave me my first acting lesson.

I never did get to drama school. I still feel I've missed out. But Ann did set me off on a decades-long, still unfinished journey of learning what acting actually is. I learnt by being in shows, by rubbing up against talented people and by doing it all wrong.

Starting with Ann's first acting lesson.

My First Acting Lesson

It was an audition for an ad for Kelvinator. Washing machines as far as I remember. Very exciting. For the first time in my life, I was going to earn money as an actor.

'Here', she said, giving me the script. 'Try this.'

It was a straight piece to camera. A presenter, if you like. I had played presenters before in sketches. I knew how to do this. I took the script and plunged in.

'The Kelvinator 500XZ is reliable and efficient.'

I was the epitome of the cool, zany, hilarious presenter. Think Michael Palin in *Monty Python*. Eyebrows and assumed voice.

Ann stopped me. 'It doesn't sound as though you believe it. You've got to genuinely believe that this washing machine is fantastic.'

This was quite a new idea. I'd never had to do that before. I started again. I took out the ironic zaniness and the eyebrows.

'The Kelvinator 500XZ is reliable and efficient.'

She stopped me again. 'Well, better, but you still don't sound as if you believe it. This is the best washing machine around. You're very excited about it. Try again.'

I tried again. I now realised what not to do, but that didn't really help. Avoiding insincerity wasn't the same as creating genuine enthusiasm. How could I generate a truthful conviction that this washing machine was fabulous? I couldn't care less about washing machines. I tried again.

'The Kelvinator 550XZ is RELIABLE *AND* EFFICIENT!!!'

Hopeless.

'It's not as easy as it looks, is it?'

'No.'

I felt like I'd stumbled on a new world, except that it seemed to be behind a closed door, and I couldn't work out how to open it.

Hamlet encounters this problem too. About how to act, I mean, not about how to open closed doors. One of the Players weeps as he describes Hecuba, the Queen of Troy, running through the burning streets of her city. Hamlet is amazed.

'What's Hecuba to him or he to Hecuba, that he should weep for her?'

How can you feel emotion for something completely separate from you? Hamlet and I were in the same philosophical dilemma. Hecuba was my Kelvinator 500XZ.

The answer is simple, although it took me 30 years to work it out. It's one word.

Empathy.

When you see two football players collide on the football field and bang heads, you wince. You can feel the thwack yourself. That's a form of empathy. You're putting yourself in the position of the footballers. It's not a particularly admirable form of empathy perhaps because it's involuntary. But it does show that we are all innately empathetic. We just need to develop it.

And that's just what an actor does. They empathise. Except they don't have the convenience of seeing what the character is going through; all they've got is the words on the page and their own imagination and experience. And ability to research.

But there's no difference between the feelings that you feel as yourself and the feelings that you feel in character.

I once saw an interview with an older Australian actor who said that it had taken him 25 years to learn to act. I can't remember who it was. The story would be more interesting if I could. I do remember feeling slightly depressed by the thought. But I think it's developing empathy that's the thing that takes that long. To be able to put yourself smack bang into the middle of the character and feel what they're feeling.

Empathy.

No-one tells Hamlet that. And no-one, sadly, at the time, told me. And surprisingly I didn't get the ad.

Ann ran acting classes. Mostly taught by acting teachers but often she took the class herself. Acting lesson number two: she took out a large marble.

'I want you to pass this around and pretend it's a cow's eyeball', she said. And we did. Everyone took it and said 'Ewww!' and looked at it in a disgusted way. My brother, who was in the class too, picked it up and put it into his eye. And said 'Moooo!' I wished I'd thought of it first.

'Alright', she said. 'What about this?'

And she took out a real cow's eye and plonked it on the table. It was fatty and fleshy and alien looking. It was frightening. The reaction was utterly different. We gasped. Some people actually screamed and stood up. It was viscerally shocking.

When I'd recovered, I looked at my brother with an air of reproach. How infantile.

But the biggest shock was seeing the difference between our attitude to the marble when we *thought* we were being real and our attitude to the real thing.

Again – there can be no difference between what the character feels in any situation and what you actually feel yourself. Otherwise you're just playing around.

And that's the hardest thing for a young actor to really come to terms with. It's easy to have an intellectual appreciation of the fact that Juliet is scared all alone, lying in that coffin, in a darkened tomb. After all, she's just about to take a potion which will render her unconscious for hours. And what is she, thirteen? Quite understandable that she'd be scared. **But you've got to be scared too.** Actually be scared. Understand the circumstances and have the emotion. That's not a marble, it's a cow's eye. It couldn't be more real.

And if that's the only thing you get from this book, then it's all been worthwhile. And if you think you have got it, then you can shut the book now and go and do something else. Job well done. Although you will miss the discussion of the No Underpants rule. And at the risk of being boring, I will say it again.

Empathy.

The Tax Office

I now had an agent, but there didn't seem to anything for her to take her ten per cent out of. Advertising whitegoods seemed a dead end and no-one wanted to audition me for anything else. I tried stand-up comedy without great success. My first gig was marred by a complete lack of attention from the audience. There was a sea of chatter from the hopeful beginning of my act to its deflated end. This was bad enough but my humiliation was compounded by the fact that I was the support act to an Elvis Presley impersonator whose idea of banter was to pause between songs and ask 'How about that stand-up? Was he any good?'

The answer to his question was a resounding and collective 'No! Shithouse!' It seemed a fairly conclusive response but it didn't seem to stop him asking. Or the audience from responding. I took my cheque from the reluctant organiser and thought to myself that it was probably the lowest I could possibly go.

About a year later, I was proven wrong. I accepted a gig to entertain a Christmas party of Master Builders. This time there was no disrespectful audience chat. I came on stage to a respectful silence, I started my act in an atmosphere of quietness, and completed it, all in the same contemplative and polite absence of noise. In fact, throughout the entirety of the half hour stream of what I thought was reasonably amusing material, there was not a single sound from the audience. At one point I thought I did hear someone mutter, 'That one wasn't bad' but I couldn't swear to it. What I was certain of was that I had managed to complete my act uncontaminated by any form of audible response. The pianist hired to play incidental music during the eating part of the night was welcomed back with loud cheering.

It was my last attempt at stand-up.

Back to square one. In desperation I took a position as a base-grade clerk in the Tax Office, filing documents. There was not enough work to last through the day, but you were not allowed to finish early and then do nothing. You had to either work slowly or look busy. It was a soul-destroying situation and I desperately wanted to leave. I can't remember a single day that I entered the building without the sinking feeling of being in prison.

But at last another audition. This time as a presenter on *Here's Humphrey*, a children's TV show featuring a bear called Humphrey. Humphrey was a person in a bear suit. He had a hat, shirt and bright yellow tie, but, slightly sinisterly, no trousers. The audition was uneventful. I waited.

And waited.

Waiting to hear about a job is one of the least attractive elements of an actor's life. You imagine yourself in the job. You've already spent the money, if not in real life, then at least in your head. You can see yourself telling your family and friends that you've got the part. You live in a very pleasant dream world where you are a successful, working actor. And that way madness lies. To make it worse, I was stuck in a low paid, unchallenging, boring job in the public service. And to make it doubly, triply, quadruply worse, Anne told me I had got to the final two. The agony of waiting and the almost-within-reach dream of telling the Tax Office to rack off and becoming a rich and famous TV presenter became unbearable. I rang Anne constantly to see if she'd heard anything. Don't do this yourself.

'I'll let you know as soon as I hear anything', she said, logically but unhelpfully. At one point I even tracked her down at her home on the weekend to ask her if anything had happened. And incurred a well-deserved lecture about **never ringing your agent on the weekend.**

The insult added to the injury of this sort of waiting is that you may never get closure. Often, you don't hear that you didn't get it, you just go on hoping until you hear second-hand that someone else has it, or, even worse, the show comes on TV with someone else in the part. And the longer you wait, the less hope you have until finally you have to accept that you're not getting it and start to climb out of the pit you dug yourself into.

The only way to cope is to forget about the audition as soon as you've done it. Tell yourself you didn't get it and go on with your life. Easier said than done. Allow yourself a moment of hopeful expectation and then put the audition away. And similarly, when and if you hear you didn't get the part, allow yourself an evening of drunken self-pity and bitterness and then get up in the morning and start again.

And finally, eventually, Ann did ring.

'I'm afraid it's bad news. They decided to go for the good-looking one.'

The last twist of the knife.

I may have spent more than one evening in the drunken self-pity stage with that one. Memory, for various reasons, is unhelpful.

As a side note, in my experience, when your agent says to you, 'You're in the final two', or 'You're the director's choice', it's really code for 'You won't get it.'

If you were everyone's first choice, you would already have been told you'd got the part. ***If you're the director's first choice, why haven't they cast you already? Because someone else – the client or the producer – doesn't like you.*** And they inevitably win. Similarly, if you're in the final two, there must be *some* issue with you or you'd be in the final one.

I did an audition for a Myers ad once. One line, as a Christmas elf, but the fee was $100,000.

I'll repeat that.

$100,000.

And I was the director's choice. For weeks and weeks. And forget about not thinking about the audition after you've done it, I was already in Paris, swanning around in a suit made from $50 notes and dining on endangered species. And of course, I didn't get it in the end, because I wasn't *everyone's* choice. If they really want you – they'll almost always tell you immediately.

But back to Humphrey.

As far as coming to terms with being the 'not good-looking one', if acting is anything it is a long and not always pleasant journey towards self-knowledge. And there's nothing like realising how people see you, via the medium of being cast as a particular part, to help you on that journey of self-knowledge. We actors really get a bit of an unfair advantage. Over the years I have found that I often get cast as idiots. Idiots and occasionally priests. And sometimes both at the same time. It used to bother me. This is what people think of me? It doesn't so much any more. I have characteristics that lead people to cast me this way. I can no more change who I am than fly to the moon.

I was once asked to audition for the ABC drama *Mercury* as a murderer with an acquired brain injury. I got the part too. 'Ah, so that's how people see me. As a mentally-retarded psychopath. Jolly good.'

But the thing to remember about being typecast is that it does involve being cast.

I Get a Job

So the empty vista of life as an unsuccessful would-be actor continued to be unbroken by the hint of any work appearing on the horizon. Meanwhile Shaun Micallef and I had got together with two amusing humans, Alex Ward and Anthony Durkin, and were continuing to perform whenever we could. Shaun wrote a show called *The Ages of Man*. It was really a collection of long sketches, ending with the Four Horsemen of the Apocalypse holding their AGM. I played, I think, War, and we finished, as these AGMs often do, with a song entitled *Grongle Grongle Wheedle Wheedle* which I played on the piano-accordion. The chorus went:

> Grongle, Grongle, Wheedle, Wheedle
> I've got a brand new pair of coconuts.
> Grongle, Grongle, Wheedle, Wheedle. *(And hold.)*
> Dean, where are you Dean?

And no – apart from a Jerry Lewis reference in the last line, it has no meaning at all.

At that time, the Artistic Director of the State Theatre Company of South Australia (STCSA) was actor John Gaden. His PA, God bless her, was a girl called Deb. She wasn't a great fan of our stuff, having already seen it when we were at uni. She didn't want to go to the show. But her friend did and so, reluctantly, she came. Presumably she was more impressed with this one, or perhaps she liked bad zydeco, because as a result of that chance attendance, she suggested to John that he audition me for a part in Shakespeare's *The Tempest*.

This is how you circumvent the catch-22 of getting an agent. **Do your own work. Do it by yourself, or get together with others and put on shows.** And then hope you get lucky and someone sees you. Eventually – probably someone will. But they certainly won't if you just sit by the phone and wait for them to call.

The part was Stephano, the drunken butler. John was to direct. I found a monologue. I practised it over and over. I got a friend to hear me. We did it indoors, and we went outside to a children's park to do it, to the bemusement of the toddlers using the equipment. I practised at home. I muttered the lines to myself while waiting to go in to the audition. No auditionee was ever better prepared.

I entered the room where I was to audition. I took a deep breath. I prepared to do my monologue.

'Sit down. Tell me about yourself', said John. I babbled something about having done stand-up, and braced myself for my monologue.

'Well, let's hear your act', he said. 'I need a good laugh.'

'Oh, God', I thought. I staggered through a greatest hits version of the least awful parts of my act. John was good enough to feign laughter.

Now, surely, I thought, he'll want to hear my monologue.

'Do you want to hear my monologue?'

'Let's have a read of the script', he said.

I read a scene carefully aloud. Pause.

'Can you do it with a bit more ... brio?'

I tried to oblige.

'Good. Rehearsals start in July. Come and I'll introduce you to the designer.'

I had already opened my mouth to insist I finally be allowed to do my monologue before the gist of what he had said hit me. And I shut up.

I've found that it's not a good idea to over-prepare. Or to lock yourself into a performance before rehearsals. Or to arrive at an audition or on set with too many preconceptions. You inevitably find that the circumstances are completely different to what you imagine. The director has found an interesting prop, a newspaper or spatula or tree that he or she wants you to read or use or climb. The other actor is doing their lines in a completely different way to the way you imagined them doing it in your head, or is standing in a different place. Even more unsettlingly, the lines may be completely rewritten on the spot, just before you shoot.

You need to arrive in an open, available state, aware that you have no idea how the scene is going to go and happy to follow where you're led.

This doesn't mean under-prepare, of course. But when you do learn your lines, learn them in a flexible way.

If I'm auditioning for a TV role, then I know I'll be in a small room with a camera pointing at me. The reader (or the casting agent if they can't afford a reader) will be standing to one side of the camera reading the lines. So, when I go through it beforehand, I imagine that the person I'm talking to is on the right of the camera, and then I change and place them on the left. Or I do it sitting and then standing. Anything to keep it flexible and open.

Just be ready to throw anything you've prepared away. You may be pleasantly surprised by what happens.

And sometimes you get the part without even doing the monologue.

I was absolutely thrilled to get my first gig. I'm not sure I've ever felt as happy as I did in those few seconds after being given the part. And it's a sad fact of the actor's life that the best moment of all is immediately after being given the part. Once rehearsals start it gets difficult. But in that moment I was absolutely over the moon.

I took leave without pay from the Tax Office and turned up for the first day of rehearsals.

The Tempest

I was hopeless right from the start. And terrified. I have never been as scared as I was the first time we rehearsed Stephano's entrance, drunk and singing. It's very difficult to be creative when you're scared and I was petrified with fear for most of the rehearsal period. I only relaxed after the first run-through with the whole cast when I realised that the scenes were funny and that I was not ruining the whole thing single-handedly. Not quite.

But almost. Despite being delighted that I was finally in a real professional play, I was slightly dissatisfied with my part. I really wanted to be Trinculo. Not Stephano. Stephano and Trinculo are the two servants who are washed ashore on the island after the shipwreck. They find Caliban, a sort of indigenous inhabitant, and make a plan to take over the island. They are a sort of double act. Except Trinculo seemed to have all the funny lines. Stephano is the straight one.

In this production Trinculo was played by the late Paul Blackwell, one of Australia's great comic actors. He had a naturalness and a unique comic manner that made audiences love him. I remember being surprised to find out he had gone to drama school – he seemed too unique and too charmingly anarchical to have been through three years of rigorous training. I had always been sceptical about acting schools (those grapes did look very sour), but I started to revise my opinion. Maybe they were a force for good after all.

But I was doing my best to ruin the double act by trying to be funny. Stephano himself is not 'funny', but his actions do contribute to the comedy. If he plays them properly. He just needs to react to what is happening in a truthful way. It's Trinculo, however, who generally gets the laughs. I was using my Footlights brain and trying to get laughs that weren't there rather than playing the scene and being part of a duo, honouring the text and getting laughs together.

I have no doubt John was concerned. I seem to recall a Saturday rehearsal being called for just Paul and me and Steven Vidler who was playing Caliban. Presumably I was straightened out at that point. It is all lost in the dark backward and abysm of time. To quote the play.

However, what I do vividly remember from that day was one of John's first directions to me. 'Really ask those questions, Francis.'

In Stephano's first scene, he enters and discovers Trinculo and Caliban sheltering from the storm under a blanket. He doesn't know what he has found.

> 'What's the matter? Have we devils here? Do you put tricks upon's with savages and men of Ind, ha?'

I was just saying the lines. Not actually properly asking the questions. But Stephano isn't just talking for the sake of talking. He genuinely thinks that he might have found devils. He's terrified at the prospect. And he really wants to know if they are or not.

Generally, if a character asks a question it's because they really want to know. You have to make sure you're really asking it. You need to be genuinely puzzled and genuinely seeking an answer. And the higher the stakes, the bigger the desire to discover.

Paul Blackwell and I were sent to costume fittings together. I was given my costume and I put it on: enormous Elizabethan breeches, shiny codpiece, shirt and waistcoat. Ken Wilby, the designer, seemed pleased. Paul was slightly less amenable.

'I've just been in a storm and I've swum to shore. My costume wouldn't look like this', he said.

He jettisoned the waistcoat. 'I lost that in the water.'

He grabbed his codpiece and bashed it so it had a dent in it. He stood on it and scraped it along the ground. He was barely prevented from ripping a hole in the breeches. I looked at Ken, he seemed no less pleased with Paul than with me. I was stunned.

But Paul was absolutely right. He'd just thought about it a bit more than I had.

Your character is your responsibility. Don't just accept what the director or designer dictate. Unless you're happy with where they're going.

The rest of the cast were all very experienced actors. I felt completely out of my depth. John Noble was playing Alonso, the King of Naples who overthrows Prospero and then loses his son in the shipwreck. He would later find fame in the *Lord of the Rings* films.

'I've discovered Alonso's stillness', I remember him saying. 'He's a very still person.'

I looked at the lines, there seemed nothing there to necessarily indicate lack of movement. I couldn't work out what he was going on about. It was a moving performance though and my first exposure to the idea that finding one's character was a mysterious business.

We eventually got into the theatre. I was sharing a dressing-room with Paul, Steven Vidler who was Caliban and Dan Witton who was Ariel. Everything was new. Everyone knew what they were doing except me.

I watched and copied. All of the cast had make-up kits, generally a fishing tackle box stuffed with make-up from previous shows. Paul had a stipple sponge, whatever that was, and a tube of blood. Steven created a broken nose effect just from two different shades of make-up. I felt inadequate. With my next pay, I went and bought a fishing tackle box and put my small and unimpressive make-up supplies inside. I felt a bit more like a real actor.

My ignorance was wide-ranging. Come the performances I naively assumed that the cast would stay in their dressing-rooms during the interval thinking about their character and the character's journey and generally being intense. During our first preview I did just that. But there was noise coming from the green room and the sound of clicking balls and when I looked out of my dressing-room I was stunned to see the whole cast making themselves cups of tea, playing pool and chatting. Nary a reflective moment or meditative silence among them. I was relieved and disappointed at the same time.

I really don't remember much about the production. I know I was terrible. I tried to be Paul Blackwell. I didn't play the moment. I was rigid with fear. Looking back over my script now, I see that a lot of my lines were cut or whittled down, so I suppose John was trying to limit the damage. I knew absolutely nothing about actors or the acting process, and I'm sure it showed. In the end if I came out of it with any credibility at all, it was because I was working with Paul. I didn't realise how lucky I was to have landed him as my first onstage partner and I owe him a big debt. His passing was a great loss.

Steven Vidler had also been cast as the Sea Captain. It's a small part – he only appears in the first scene as the ship is hit by a storm. Presumably he dies in the shipwreck. A few days into the run, Steven lost his voice from shouting over the storm sound effects. I was co-opted to replace him. A few days later I lost my voice too.

We ended up alternating the Sea Captain to preserve our voices, and that seemed to work, but I learned from the experience that 'projection' is not 'shouting' and the good actors can speak apparently quite calmly and quietly but still hit the back wall of the theatre. A dying art owing to the intrusion of radio mikes into the theatre but more on that anon.

One final memory. Teddy Hodgman, one of South Australia's hidden treasures, was playing Prospero. I had grown up watching Teddy on stage. I'd seen him in the title role in the Scottish play. And now I was on stage with him. I can still hear him say the lines. I hardly dared address two words to him. Although I found out in later shows he could be very naughty and had a wicked sense of humour.

One notes session, I found myself sitting next to him. He leaned over and whispered, 'You're getting the stress wrong on one of your lines. Can I show you?' He wrote the line on my script 'I was the man in the moon' and underlined the word 'man'. 'Do you see?' I nodded. I've never followed a note more conscientiously. Poor man, he had sat and listened wincing for over a month before he could bear it no longer.

I still have the script, with Teddy Hodgman's note written on the inside cover. He was a wonderful Prospero. Usually our childhood heroes turn out to have feet of clay. Mine did not.

As the season drew on, many in the cast started to get twitchy.

'I'll be glad when this is over.' 'Looking forward to finishing.' Et cetera.

Some had another play lined up, some were going to have a holiday. This is just what happens. No matter how long or short the job, it seems just one week too long and it's often hard to get to the end. And the quite intense bond you've formed with these people, whom you've gone into battle with, is dissolved and you say goodbye and you may not see them again for ten years, if at all. It's a very bitter-sweet element of the industry.

I, however, was not looking forward to finishing at all. I was just going back to the Tax Office. There seemed to be no path for me to another job. Like Moses, I had been shown the Promised Land but told I would never get there. And while the analogy may seem somewhat overblown, I can assure you that, if anything, it underplays the anguish of the actor whose first job also seemed his last.

Alice in Wonderland

I returned to the Tax Office. It was as if I had never left. People kept saying to me, 'You won't be here for long'. They meant well, but I couldn't see any way out of the place, and their cheery assurance only made me more depressed. I had no idea what my next step was. I hung around the STCSA whenever I could find a reason to, principally seeing shows I wasn't in and going to the theatre bar.

And it was while I was there, palely loitering and toying with a moody beer, that Deb, John Gaden's PA, found me.

'Has your agent rung you?'

'No?'

'You've got some good news coming.'

And there was. Magpie, the youth theatre wing of the SA State Theatre Company was putting on a production of *Alice in Wonderland* and I was offered a part. I was to play Tweedledee, the Mad Hatter and various other roles. I took more leave without pay. And I entered the separate universe of youth theatre.

Magpie was a wonderful company, sometimes doing shows in theatres, but often going into schools. I remember seeing them myself – in fact, any young South Australian who aspired to act had probably been nudged in that direction by seeing a Magpie show.

I loved doing youth theatre – there is generally less ego amongst its practitioners and a truer and more genuine response from its audience. This youthful honesty, however, is not all roses, and I rapidly discovered that young audiences will not hesitate to communicate their dissatisfaction with your work if it doesn't meet their standards. The questions after the show were usually direct and to the point.

'Don't you get embarrassed?'

'Why is your nose so big?'

And once, inexplicably, 'Are you lesbians?'

At any rate, I was working again. It was the end of 1989 and I had managed to get that tricky second job. It's one thing to get initial employment as an actor, it's quite another thing to continue to get work.

I turned up to rehearsals, a little less terrified and a little more aware of what the whole thing was about.

I noticed on the first day of rehearsals, as was the case with *The Tempest*, that everyone seemed to have highlighted their lines with a highlighter pen. So they wouldn't miss any, I suppose. And like clockwork, every time scripts are handed out, in any cast I've ever been in, there's a flurry of activity as actors inevitably get out their highlighters and go through the script highlighting their lines.

I understand this, it's a way of starting work on the script. There's my part, all coloured in. I'm on the way.

But although I was very much in a copying and learning phase, I didn't copy this. And I never have. It seems to me that it puts too much emphasis on what you're saying. The play/film/TV show isn't just about you after all and you will be doing something while the others are saying their lines, I hope. Listening to them and being changed by what is said. And that listening is just as, if not more, important than your lines.

Highlighting leads you down the path of thinking that if you have your lines under control then you've done your job. And that your lines are more important than the others. But they're not. ***All of those lines have the same importance, so why are you highlighting just yours?*** If you don't highlight, you'll still be okay. You probably won't miss your lines in rehearsal if you're on the ball and, even if you do, someone will say 'Francis, it's you' and the sky won't fall in. Despite the momentary puzzlement as to why someone's calling you Francis.

It was during this production that I first came across the No Underpants rule. The No Underpants rule is not often imposed. It is fairly self-explanatory. It forbids the use of underpants under the costume so as not to destroy the line of the trouser or because, in Elizabethan England, for example, brightly coloured boxers would be anachronistic. In my case the costume consisted of a loose sort of a onesie made of a flimsy material and it was feared that the underpants would be evident through the garment and ruin the effect.

The problem that subsequently arose, however, and this will be immediately apparent to anyone with a knowledge of anatomy and soft fabrics, was that if the underpants is not evident, then certain other things will be.

At one point during this production I was required to advance to the front of the stage (or rather the playing area, since the seats were on the same level as the performing space, bringing the audience's eyes roughly to the level of our groins) and do a sort of little jiggy dance. It will be immediately apparent where this is headed.

Because the problem with doing a sort of little jiggy dance in a loose onesie sans undergarments is that one's arms and legs are not the only things participating in the jigging. And, moreover, when one's arms and legs stop jigging, it takes a moment or two for these other things to cotton on to the fact that the jigging has stopped and so, in fact, should they.

Now I enjoy a bit of choreography. It's hugely satisfying to work on a routine, get it into one's bones and then to be able to go on stage in front of an audience and just go with the music. It's a less satisfying experience, unsurprisingly, when, although your upper body and legs are behaving as they should, it's testicles akimbo in the middle. And satisfying is not even remotely appropriate as a descriptor if you have to perform this dance, as I had to one matinee, to a party of Year 6 Loreto schoolgirls in the front row, eyes at groin level (or a mean of the groin level, taking into account the fluctuations of the body parts in question), while the girls shrieked with that hysterical and embarrassed shrieky laughter that only a 12-year-old girl is capable of.

I had already learnt that your costume is your own responsibility during *The Tempest*. But it's easy to forget lessons you learn just by watching. It's not so easy to forget them when the learning process involves intense humiliation in the matter of one's pink bits. And it's a good lesson. ***Any decision about costume, design or script is a decision about me. I have to wear it, so to speak, and consequently I must not just accept what the director or designer decides if I*** *don't agree with it.* And if I don't agree with it, then I need to make my case clearly and politely.

A lesson the rest of the cast, more experienced than me, had already learnt. When the No Underpants rule was first announced, they just laughed and continued to wear underpants. And no young girls pointed at their groins and laughed. Which is just as it should be.

About halfway through the run, the audiences started to dwindle. In many respects *Alice in Wonderland* isn't really suited to children. There are some quite adult philosophical concepts and a few too many parodies of Victorian songs, and our production, for this or other reasons, failed to fire. In desperation the publicity department turned their attention to the other end of the age spectrum and buses of faintly protesting old age pensioners started to arrive for the matinees.

I do not think these senior citizens enjoyed the show any more than the children. In fact, I am sure of it, since one matinee, as we were proceeding on our unimpressive way through the show, one elderly lady could bear it no longer and her quavering yet extremely audible voice was heard above our dialogue: 'I don't like him!'

The whole theatre froze.

There were four of us on stage at the time, three males and Alice. There was safety to be had in numbers. Certainly, this was embarrassing, but if we could just ignore the interruption and continue then no harm had been done. And it could be any one of the three of us she was referring to. In fact, it was almost certainly one of the other two, they'd gone downhill a bit since opening night, and my personal charm, I'd long believed, was considerable. And I'm sure the other two were thinking exactly the same thing. And anyway, perhaps no-one had noticed.

We drew breath to continue and put it all behind us but it was not to be. There's no Laurel without Hardy, no Bert without Ernie and no irritable elderly audient without her similarly aged and slightly less with-it companion. 'Which one?' came the no less audible question from another senior citizen, seated next to her. We all died a little inside.

'Him!' came the swift and inexorable response. 'The one with the dark curly hair. I don't like him!'

It goes without saying that I was the only one with dark curly hair on stage. It was certainly obvious to the rest of the audience, who could see the hair for themselves, but if there was any doubt in anyone's mind, a thin bony finger was quite clearly pointed in my direction.

The show trudged its way to the end, but the high point had already been reached. For my part, I had to continue to perform with the knowledge that not only did one member of the audience dislike my performance or my person so much that she felt compelled to express her feelings out loud, but also that the rest of the audience were now examining me closely to work out in exactly what respect I was unlikeable and, no doubt, coming to the conclusion that the old lady had a point.

I'm not sure what the lesson is here. I just needed to get it off my chest. Probably resilience. Just as I had to go on dancing and smiling, as though I was having the time of my tiny life, while young girls pointed at my groin and giggled, and just as I had to go on with the show after having been publicly humiliated, so one has to put one's personal feelings, of sadness or resentment or existential angst or whatever, aside once the show starts. No-one cares what you're personally going through when you're on stage. Except your mother. And she's probably not that interested either. It can't and it mustn't affect the performance. **The audience have paid to see the show. Not how your day has affected you.**

Kafka's Dick

Another show finished. Again, nothing on the horizon. I returned to Adelaide University to take a part in an early play by Alan Bennett, the enigmatically entitled *Kafka's Dick*. Kafka comes back to life after asking his best friend, Max Brod, to burn all his writing. To his chagrin, he finds that he's a famous author. Hilarity ensues. Shaun Micallef directed it.

I played Kafka-bore Sydney, into whose home Kafka inexplicably intrudes. It's an amusing play with a great book-hiding set piece in which Sydney and Brod hide all the books about Kafka, so that Kafka won't see them and realise he's a literary giant. We practised and practised until it became a slapstick masterpiece. That's the way I remember it anyhow.

One of the actors was leaving a large gap after my line before he came in with his own. It dragged the energy of the play down and meant that the audience was ahead of us, waiting for us to catch up, rather than being led by us. It also gave the impression that something was wrong, that perhaps someone had forgotten their line. And worst of all, it seemed as though it was my fault.

If you feel the scene's not going well, try picking up your cues.

I asked him to be a bit quicker off the mark, but his performance was set and no amount of rehearsing or pleading could change this.

In the end, in slight desperation and without telling him, I resorted to tricking him into it. I would set a reasonably fast pace on my line and then suddenly break the rhythm by slowing down suddenly at the end. My colleague, expecting the line to finish earlier than it did, would say his line in his own good time, only to find that he was actually coming in hard on his cue. I don't recommend you try this at home. And anyway, it didn't always work.

However, what did become clear to me was that ***you can't change someone else's performance,*** you can only deal with what's in front of you and try to make it work for you.

As I started to work with professional actors, who could more readily change their performances at will, I modified this.

Don't ever try to change someone else's performance, just adapt your own.

It's a very tricky thing to give another actor direction. However it's couched and however friendly the two of you are, it always comes across as slightly annoying. Of course, if the actor has asked you for help, that's a different matter.

And you can always suggest ideas. 'You might get a laugh if you say the line *before* picking up the sausages.' But even then, you need to be careful.

But asking someone to change their performance to suit you, 'Could you not move during my line? It destroys a moment I'm trying to achieve', is a recipe for disaster. That's the director's job. You'll just irritate the other actor and destroy any rapport that may be building between the two of you.

On another note, a theatrical production, like anything, is never completely right. There will always be moments in someone else's performance, or in the direction of the scene, that you feel are wrong. That irritate you. Tough cheese. It's not your show. You have to put up with them. And no-one's perfect. Not even you.

Evensong for Antarctica

And finally another job. In 1991 I was cast in another youth theatre piece, this one called *Evensong for Antarctica*. I played a sensitive, clarinet-playing teenager who is deeply affected by the plight of harp seals. David Sadler, coincidentally the good-looking one who got the Humphrey gig, played my brother. I tried to resent him. Unfortunately he was as pleasant as he was good-looking and I couldn't.

At one stage during this well-meaning but over-worthy play, I was required to watch a sealer miming the action of clubbing harp seals to death and burst into floods of tears.

Crying on stage was something I'd never ever had to do before. I didn't know where to start. I couldn't have cared less about harp seals. Sure it was sad they got killed but it was all a little abstract to get upset over. And it wasn't as if they were there. We didn't have the budget. So I had to bring them into being and then get upset about their demise? This was silly.

And I come back to the answer to Hamlet's question – professional empathy.

At the time, of course I was in no position to have even articulated the issue. And as for being able to put it into use, forget about it. It took me years to get it. And I'm still not completely on top of it now.

Suffice to say that way back then, my young self, untrained, new to the stage and with no life experience to speak of (in other words, completely unequipped to use my own experiences and emotions to serve the given circumstances of the play and produce something truthful and felt), did what most actors do in this situation. *I faked it.* I put my head down and screwed up my eyes and made crying sounds.

And that's fine.

Sometimes you can't get it. You haven't done the work beforehand, it's not working for you that day, the writing doesn't make sense, whatever. It just won't gel. You've still got to do it, whether the performance is emotionally connected or not. This is the JFD theory of acting as a director once explained to me. Just f...... do it.

The audience will generally do a lot of the work for you. If they're engaged in the story they'll fill in the emotion themselves even if it's not there. Just look at film actors – beautiful wooden faces, perfect for a close-up, no need for any thoughts or emotions behind the facade. They just stand in front of the camera. The audience, the editing and the music do the job for them.

It is possible I'm being a bit hard on film actors. You may notice if you peruse my CV that there's not a lot of film there. But I'm not bitter.

At any rate, a lot of this is bluff. *If you're not feeling it on the day, just fake it until you do.* And 90 per cent of the audience won't notice any difference. But you have to do *something*. That's the job. Like pretending to cry.

And a curious thing happened in my case. As the show went on I found I was becoming more and more emotional in the seal clubbing scene. The physical act of crying was beginning to make me feel like crying. There's a sort of two-way street going on here. If you believe you are cold, your body will start to feel cold and to take on the physical appearance of a body that's cold. Shoulders hunched over, perhaps the arms cradling the body, et cetera. But equally, if you take the physical shape a cold person makes, then you will start to feel cold as well. The body follows the mind, but the mind also follows the body.

So sometimes, just faking it is a pathway into gradually feeling it.

But whatever, the first step is doing it.

And in case you didn't know, the word 'actor' comes from the Greek word for 'doing'. Not 'talking', or even 'feeling', but 'doing'. An actor does. And in fact, whenever I direct, I always have the same response when an actor comes to me with an idea.

'No.'

Sorry, couldn't resist. The response is actually 'Show me.' I don't want to hear about it, and I don't want to discuss it. I want to see you do it, and then we'll be able to see immediately if it works or not.

The reviews for *Evensong for Antarctica* weren't kind. One sentence remains with me: 'Francis Greenslade's awkward breathy clarinet playing caused the woman in front of me to search frantically in her handbag for a cough lozenge.'

And while I unreservedly apologise to the unnamed theatre-goer for exacerbating her throat condition, I can't help thinking that that's a bit mean.

Wind in the Willows

Little by little I began to get more work. That same year there was an outdoors production of *Wind in the Willows* coming to Adelaide. I auditioned for it.

'Can you do your piece again', asked the director, 'as if you were a strong powerful animal?'

'Aha!' I thought. 'I'm auditioning for Badger. I'll do it like a badger.'

And I did the piece like a badger would. You've never seen a more badger-like version of Rosencrantz's box speech. Menacing, powerful. Badgerish.

The next day Ann rang me.

'He wants you for Otter.'

Otter, Badger. Potato, potahto.

Again, I applied for more leave without pay from the Tax Office. This time it was denied. 'We can't afford to keep losing staff. If you want to do this show, you'll have to resign.' Sound of slamming door, running feet, car starting up and accelerating away. And I was free.

And that was the last 'real job' I ever had.

It's extremely difficult to survive in Australia solely as an actor. I managed it by a combination of luck, relying on government assistance and being extremely poor for long periods of time. Luck is unreliable and the dole is now much harder to get and comes with so many strings attached it's almost not worth it. So we're left with being extremely poor. Which is very reliable and quite easy to access.

The other alternative, of course, is getting a job. David Mamet says that he's delighted when he hears of an actor getting a non-acting job. It means that eventually that actor will find themselves doing that job full-time and the serious actors will have a more open playing field.

This is a bit unfair. One has to eat. But he does have a point underneath the unreasonableness. I once met an actor in a bookshop. He was working there.

'I haven't had an acting job for six years', he told me sadly.

I sympathised. No, I empathised. There but for the grace of God. But I did wonder at what point he would stop referring to himself as an actor and start telling people he sold books.

It's a tricky situation. If you do take a job to survive, the danger is that it starts to be the main event and acting gets squeezed out. On the other hand, you have to be very lucky or very good, or both, to manage just on performing.

My costume as Otter was simple. A wetsuit. At the start of the play I would secrete myself in a bush near the audience, at the side of the lake we were performing around, and wait until I could hear my cue approaching. Au moment juste, I would slide into the water and half paddle half crawl along the bank towards the audience, subsequently leaping up with the cry 'Hello Rabbits!' It was, all things considered, a good entrance. One afternoon, as I was making my way through the water, I disturbed a small turtle, who rapidly swam away. 'How nice to be at one with nature' was my thought at the time.

I was considerably less serene a few shows later, when I had to avoid a hypodermic needle floating along. I later found out that the lake was fed by Adelaide's stormwater drains and my appetite for water-based entrances diminished appreciably.

At some point during the run, Adelaide decided to put on a heatwave. Temperatures were regularly over 40 degrees. The children who came would become fretful and start to cry. It got very difficult to do the show, especially as there were two a day, one at 11:00 and the second at 3:00.

The cast got together to discuss this. This was in the days before OH&S and there were no guidelines set down for the comfort and safety of the actors. We decided we would not work if the temperature went above 43 degrees and we would not do two shows in a day if the temperature was over 40. Eminently reasonable, we thought. I believe the rules now are much stricter.

One among us was deputised to go and talk to management, which they duly did. And sadly, I can't remember whether we actually did have to cancel shows after that. What I do remember is being told, some time after the show had finished, that as a consequence of our deputy going to see them, the producers decided that that particular actor would never work for them again. And to the best of my knowledge, they never did.

And this is why you need to join the union.

If it wasn't for the Actors' Equity, the union that represents actors, we would still be providing our own costumes. We would not be paid for rehearsing, there would be no restrictions on how long we could work without a break, no award minimum, no allowances for living away from home, no payment for online content and certainly no rules for the wellbeing of actors working outdoors. The union continually renegotiates actor's wages and conditions so they don't fall behind cost of living increases, and perhaps most importantly they take the emotion out of any disputes, so that no-one shoots the messenger.

They also negotiate from a position of some strength. Equity are a strong union. Over the last 30 years, union membership in Australia has dropped from approximately 40 per cent to 15 per cent of the workforce, but in the acting industry the figure is much much higher. It's difficult to give it a figure, but on most TV and stage shows that I've worked on it's easily over 90 per cent. And this gives it its strength. Union action is very, very rarely taken, but, because most of the workforce are members of the union, the consequences of it being taken are so drastic that the threat of action is usually enough.

And it gives a feeling of belonging. This industry is very fragmented. You work with someone for a couple of months and then you may never see them again. There aren't many professional events where actors get together. Perhaps you might see someone at a show or an awards night, but that's about it.

That little card, however, that says you're a member of Equity, that's a badge. It says that you belong to this extraordinary group of extraordinary people. And over and above the many practical reasons for joining, it's very comforting to feel that you're part of the gang.

Magpie

I had a handful of professional shows under my belt. There seemed little prospect of any more. Then I heard on the grapevine that Magpie were auditioning. There was a new Artistic Director, a man called Steven Gration, and he wanted a permanent ensemble. It would be a year's contract with a possibility of an extension. This was exciting news, but it did mean that the whole of the Adelaide acting profession would be auditioning. And although Adelaide is not as big as Melbourne or Sydney, it did have two training institutions – Flinders Uni and the Centre for the Performing Arts – that popped out dozens of actors year after year, so the number of actors in Adelaide was quite large. My chances as an untrained and relatively inexperienced actor seemed absolutely nil. And to add to the impossibility of the whole exercise, three of the ensemble of five had already been hired. There were only two positions available. One male and one female.

The first audition was a group audition. These are awful things. You want to stand out, but the whole point of the exercise is to show how well you work with other people, so you can't. But you have to. Tricky.

I arrived in a vast room with what seemed like hundreds of other people. We did a group warm up. We were put into groups to create little scenes. Those of us with instruments were made to jam. The low point of the whole process. We were then given sheets of paper and crayons. Music was played. One of the lucky actors already in the ensemble danced and we were instructed to draw our impressions of her movements. I covered the page with enigmatic scrawlings and glumly remembered what my Art teacher had said to me when assessing my attempt at perspective in Year 8. 'That's … very nice paper, Francis.'

At no point in the process did I distinguish myself in any way. The final ignominy came at the end when gym mats were set out and Steven started teaching us to cartwheel.

I couldn't cartwheel. I still can't. My secret theory is that like brown eyes and the ability to wiggle one's ears, I just don't have the gene for it.

And I knew that in the 30 minutes or so left before the end of the session I would not learn to cartwheel or get close to cartwheeling, or even improve slightly on my inept version of a cartwheel. Which is something like a crab being swept up in a slight current.

However, if I'd got one thing out of my gig in *Evensong for Antarctica*, it was the professional advantages of faking it and for those next 30 minutes I played the part of one determined to cartwheel, even if he was going to kill himself in the process. I did my crab impression, looked disappointed and went round for another go. And another. And another. And at the end, when Steven said 'All right. I think we'll wind up. Does anyone want one more go?' I stuck my hand up and had one more determined and inevitably doomed attempt.

Steven told me later that when he came to compile the list of those who had made it into the second round of auditions, it was only that last final attempt at a cartwheel that got me through. That he'd been impressed by my determination. Because the rest of my audition had been woeful. And he must have been really, *really* impressed with my feigned never-say-die attitude, because he'd seen me sit and pretend to cry about invisible harp seals.

So I got a call-back.

I didn't want to go to the second audition. I knew I wouldn't get it. I remember getting to the bottom of the stairs leading to the audition room and almost turning around and going home. Every actor in Adelaide was going for this job. I hadn't trained, I'd been in four, count them, four shows. And I'd been pretty bad in at least three of them. I'd caused a member of the audience to denounce me in the middle of a show. Schoolgirls had laughed at me. Critics had derided my musicianship. I was not even good-looking. There was no way I was going to get the gig.

It would have been embarrassing not to turn up, however, so I decided I'd just go in anyway. For the experience. Because I had no chance of being chosen. And I wasn't just saying this. I meant it. I knew without any doubt whatsoever, that I was not getting this job. I gloomily ascended the stairs and did the audition.

Two weeks later Deb rang me.

'How would you like to work with Magpie?'

I have absolutely no doubt that I got cast not because I was the best person for the job, but because I had absolutely no belief in my chances and therefore had absolutely nothing riding on what I did.

Auditions are inescapable. Like head lice or regrets, depending on whether or not you've left primary school. And most people hate them.

So how do we deal with them?

A lot of it is attitude. When you first get an audition it is very difficult not to visualise yourself in the job. As I did with *Here's Humphrey*. You imagine you're doing the role. You can see yourself telling your family and friends that you're going to be working on such and such, with Whatsisname, and you probably spend the money in your head several times.

But there are two problems here.

First of all, the best way to approach an audition is to focus on what you need to do for the audition. 'I need to learn the lines by Wednesday. I'll go into the casting office on Tuesday to read the whole script and I might have a Skype session with a voice coach to smarten up my Estonian accent.' If you're thinking about the job, however, you're necessarily focusing on something beyond the audition. And that's not helpful. **Forget about the role. Think about the audition.**

But secondly, the more you think about the role and the more you want it, the more dangerous the audition is. It becomes the thing standing between you and the job. It becomes a risk. It's important not to stuff up. It's *very* important not to stuff up. It's *vitally* important that you do this audition well, because you really, really want the part. And this prevents you from doing your best work. The more you want the part, the more likely you are to freeze up and make a mistake, and the more that mistake will throw you when you make it. It's as if, when you tell yourself 'Don't stuff up', the brain only hears the last two words.

The Australian rower Sally Robbins was rowing in the final of the 2004 women's eight rowing competition in the Olympics when she gave up, dropped her oar and lay back on her teammate's lap.

There is a story, perhaps apocryphal, that Sally had done this before, and that consequently her teammates had made a sign saying 'Don't Collapse' and attached it to the back of the rower in front of her.

I can think of nothing more likely to ensure that Sally collapsed than a sign containing the word 'Collapse' in her view during the race. It's stressing exactly the wrong thing. It would have been much better to have something like 'Compete', 'Endure' or 'You're strong'. Perhaps even 'Nearly wine time'.

Footballers often have words written on their arms or hands to remind them of something during the game. Often it's 'Run'. I don't believe they ever write 'Don't fall over' or 'Avoid non-competitiveness'.

So how do we avoid thinking about the delights of the job and the consequences of stuffing up while staying focused on the task at hand, i.e. the audition?

Well, lets look at what an audition actually is.

An audition is an exercise where you are given a script, or choose one yourself, and you go and perform it in front of one or more people.

As opposed to a play or a TV show or film, where you are given a script, or choose one yourself, and you go and perform it in front of one or more people.

So essentially, they're the same thing.

And when we look at it that way, it becomes hard to understand why we wouldn't like them. They're just another opportunity to perform.

And this, I think, is the key to dealing with auditions.

Presumably we chose the profession of actor because we enjoy the process. We like delivering scripts in front of an audience. It's fun.

So perhaps we should look at an audition as a chance to perform in front of an audience. The thing we most want to do.

There will be someone in the room listening to us and then

they'll probably give us a direction or two. It'll be a bit like a theatre game.

The director might even be there and then we have a chance to impress someone who's in the industry. To show off a bit. And for God's sake, it's a bit of attention. Isn't that fundamentally why we're actors at all? And now because we're not focusing on the job, but on the audition itself, it becomes something to look forward to. And we increase our chances of doing well.

I always tell myself I don't have a chance. I'm not right for the part or not a big enough name. As I did for the Magpie audition. The fact that I genuinely believed it in that case gave me an absolute freedom to just be in the room and do the audition.

And then I just look forward to doing a bit of acting and impressing the director. It won't be any use this time, because I'm not going to get the part, but perhaps he'll remember me later. And it'll be fun.

Jason Langley, the director, always tells young actors to think of the audition as the first day of rehearsals. A slightly different way of looking at it, but it takes away that desperation and need to be cast.

And it's important to remember that no audition is useless, even if you don't get the part.

Another good way to demystify auditions, if you can wangle it, is to get some work as a reader. You'll sit there all day, reading the same scenes to a series of auditionees, but it does give one a very different perspective of the audition process.

One valuable thing I got out of doing this was the realisation that auditioning actors is a bit of a chore. There's a lot of repetition involved in seeing people for the same roles all day and giving them the same spiel. So, be professional and efficient, and if you can make it interesting for them – a bit of chat, a joke – they'll appreciate it.

But once you've done your pieces, get out. Don't hang around chewing the fat. They've got more people to see and the longer you delay them, the later it'll be before they get home. Best not to irritate the director.

And don't beat yourself up. Sometimes you leave an audition thinking 'I absolutely nailed that. They loved me', but *almost inevitably you will make a mistake or two,* or miss a note you wanted to hit. It will never be as good as you did it at home. ***This mistake will not make any difference to whether or not you get the part, but how you let the mistake affect you probably will***. Let it go. You've made your mistake, that monkey's off your back and you can now get on with the rest of the audition.

So there we are. Farewell fear of auditions, hello whatever the opposite is. No need to worry about auditions anymore.

Except for self-tests. They're stupid.

The Ensemble

I now found myself in effectively permanent employment. The Magpie ensemble were hired on a yearly basis. The expectation was that we would rehearse two or three shows a year and tour them to schools. There were workshops with visiting tutors, mask work, Balinese dance, percussion. After the initial nerves it was an utterly wonderful experience and an extraordinary piece of luck.

Steven Gration was an energetic, generous creative spirit. I have never forgotten his mantra, which he often brought out when it seemed that something was wrong with the scene and we might have to jettison it and start again: **'You can make anything work.'**

This was the opposite of what I thought. If something didn't work then it needed to be thrown out and something else attempted. But the idea that you could, just by perseverance and an open mind, make anything work was quite revolutionary. Many years later I found myself doing a public debate on a team with the redoubtable singer, director and force of nature, Robyn Archer.

'I'm going to sing the *Internationale* and get the audience to join in', she said. 'You can sing it too.' 'This is going to be awful', I thought. 'You are going to die a death and take me down with you.'

I nodded glumly.

But there was never any inkling in Robyn's mind that the moment wouldn't work and, when it came to it, the enthusiasm of this extraordinarily positive human being carried the moment, the audience went with her and it was a triumph.

You can make anything work. I've held this idea in my mind over the last 30 years. I think, on balance, Steven and Robyn are probably right.

There's something very liberating about working with a director who has chosen you. Who, therefore, likes what you do and trusts you.

It gives you a feeling of safety and puts you in a place where you feel able to risk anything. It's a feeling I came to have with Steven. On the other side of the coin, it's always slightly awkward when you work with a director who, for whatever reason, didn't cast you. There's always a constraint, a feeling that perhaps they don't like my work, and it's harder to create freely. A feeling to be put aside, as it doesn't help the work, but nonetheless a feeling that exists.

I came across this much later, when cast in one of the main roles in Neil Simon's *The Odd Couple*. In contrast to the usual practice, Shaun and I were cast first and then the director, Peter Houghton, came on board. Or rather his name was suggested to us and we enthusiastically agreed. So I never auditioned for him and he never cast me in the role. He did a brilliant job and there was never any hint that he didn't like what we were doing, but the thought was always there. To be dealt with, to be disregarded, but still never completely gone. I found out later that Peter was dealing with the fact that it wasn't completely his show. Because he had been brought in after us. So I suppose there are two sides to these things. But best to acknowledge them and move on.

An ensemble is a wonderful thing when done right. There is the opportunity to create a unified method of working and a rapport between you all and you become very close very quickly. Too close sometimes. And this is the other side of the coin. I eventually started a relationship with the dancing girl from the first audition, (something you wouldn't have gleaned from the rat's nest of scribble that was my first impression of her), and suddenly an ensemble of five became a couple and three others. Which was even more problematic when you consider that, of the other three, one was married to the director.

Working with your partner can be positive and it can be negative. For me, most of the time it was extremely positive. When both relationships ended, however, it did make work difficult. And extremely tense and unpleasant at times. The nadir for me was finding myself in the middle of an oval at the Showgrounds during the Royal Show as the back end of a pantomime dog. She was the front. I hadn't realised it before, but apparently, in pantomime dog world, the person at the front end of the animal is the person that directs the action, and the half hour or so where I was ordered to sit, stand, walk and urinate by someone with whom I was not as close as I had used to be, at least emotionally, is a memory I cannot bring back without twitching.

It's a truth universally acknowledged that you shouldn't shit in your own backyard. Easy to say, but excretion is a natural and necessary bodily function and one's backyard is so very convenient. We are only human and the heart knows not the reason et cetera. So I wouldn't necessarily advise against cast relationships. They have been known to turn into lifetime arrangements. But be aware you will possibly pay for it at some point down the track. It may not come in the form of having to share a smelly poodle costume but if you do start a relationship with an actor you are working with, you need to be aware of the possibility or indeed the likelihood that it's going to end badly.

Prince of Numbskulls

One of the first shows we were to do was *Prince of Numbskulls*, a Commedia play using masks, and Steven started to expose us to trance mask work. It's described well, as so many things are, in Keith Johnstone's extraordinary book, *Impro*. I found this challenging and confronting. Strike that. I found this scary.

Steven would wait until the end of the day, when we were tired and our defences were down, and then he'd bring out his collection of masks. We would choose a mask and put it on. Steven stood behind us with a mirror. When we were ready we would turn around and look at our reflections.

The first time I did this was quite startling.

Looking into a mirror and seeing a face that's not your own is an extraordinary experience. You get shocked into a light trance. You're someone else. Initially you find yourself unable to do anything because you're frozen in shock. And in fact, for the first couple of times, Steven just let us look at ourselves and get used to our new faces.

Then, as we got used to our appearance, Steven would encourage us to make sounds and then start to speak, and a character would emerge. Without any conscious invention on our part. There was a routine that we needed to observe every time. Almost a ritual. Put the mask on, adjust it and then don't touch it again. When we were ready: 'Turn around.' Then when he saw we'd had enough: 'Turn around and take off the mask.' The same words every time.

Not touching the mask is a good general rule when doing mask work. You destroy the illusion. And, if you're doing non-trance mask work, the mask must be constantly in motion. As soon it is not, it just becomes a lifeless thing.

As I said, I had a significant degree of fear around this, both that I would not be able to do it, and also what my trance self would do, that I might lose control of it. In the beginning I chose a black, rather hostile looking mask to work with and I started to have nightmares about an unknown man dressed in dark clothes trying to get into my house. I remember watching him from inside the house, through the window in the door. And the door was, strangely enough, light blue. Exactly the same colour as the frame of the mirror that Steven was using. So the man trying to get in was … You work it out.

However, slowly but surely, we all got better at mask work and less fearful of it. I switched to a different mask, Pantalone, the old man of the Commedia dell'Arte, and I seemed to have more of an affinity with this mask. Perhaps it wasn't so threatening. At any rate, the dreams stopped.

Steven then asked Shaun Micallef to be involved. He had seen *The Ages of Man* too. The idea was that Shaun would write a script based on the characters that were emerging from the mask work.

He came to rehearsals to watch. Unfortunately it was quite early on in the process, our characters were all in their infancy and we hadn't got much beyond making incoherent noises. Shaun watched in polite bemusement as a succession of actors looked in a mirror and made grunting sounds. I think I may have stolen a biscuit. I must have been quite advanced. I could see him thinking, 'How do I make a play out of that?'

He expressed polite enthusiasm, went away and wrote a hilarious script full of Micallefesque rapid-fire witticisms and surreal gags. Unfortunately, our characters could at this point only just speak English and they were certainly not up to the verbal gymnastics that a Shaun Micallef script requires. In the end it proved too difficult for our characters to say the lines, and, when it came to performing the show, we had to abandon the trance work and revert to just wearing the masks and doing the lines as ourselves.

A pity.

I found the whole process very challenging and I didn't think I was making any progress with my Pantalone mask at all. Then after one of my sessions, one of the other actors came up to me.

'You know, every time you have that mask on, your fingers start to curl up, like claws. Something's happening there.'

This was very heartening news. I was entering the character and something new was being born. On some unconscious level I was creating something real. I could do trance work!

But that knowledge destroyed everything. After that moment, every time I put the mask on, I would check my fingers to make sure they were curling up and I lost the abandonment of self-consciousness that the mask work needed. I became too aware of what I was doing and less able to inhabit the character, let alone walk up and down the stage with a small scooter chained to my leg declaiming at a mile a minute, as Shaun's script demanded.

When we move about in the world and especially when we are involved in doing something – talking, feeling a strong emotion, concentrating on a physical task – we are very rarely aware of what we look like from the outside. There are moments when we are self-conscious, of course, but generally, at times of stress or high emotion or conflict, we are simply and purely reacting to what's happening to us and are oblivious to the way our nostrils are flaring or the shape of our mouth as we cry.

The theatre is precisely about those moments of high tension or conflict. They are its bread and butter and when we perform we are in some way trying to create a truthful representation of a human in those circumstances. **So self-awareness is not our friend.**

Obviously, there is always a little part of ourselves that is monitoring what's going on: 'Don't go any further, you'll fall off the stage.' 'Wait for that laugh.' 'The scooter has got caught on a bit of the set. You'll have to deal with it' and so on. But it's only a small part of us. The more we can lose ourselves in the action, the better. As a general rule.

However, self-consciousness seems to be the bedrock of some teaching institutions. Nowadays, due to the extraordinary explosion of film and TV work over the last twenty years, there is a plethora of small TV and film training schools whose *modus operandi* seems to be to film the students and then show them the results of their work.

I can think of nothing less conducive to acquiring a truthful method of working than to be constantly reminded of what you look like when you talk and move. It won't breed honest and truthful acting, it'll only promote self-consciousness, stereotypes and empty gesture. There may be, I'll concede, some technical benefit in correcting some mistake or other, but at what cost? Especially early in training when we're impressionable and still learning. I am old and ugly enough now to be able to watch myself on screen, and it can be useful. But I inevitably end up feeling self-conscious and deeply dissatisfied with my appearance, and that completely offsets what small practical advantage I might gain and so I do it as little as I can. **When we cry, we're not thinking about our appearance, we're thinking about the things that are making us cry. So how can it help us, when we're trying to reproduce such a moment, to be aware of what we look like?**

Prince of Numbskulls was an uneasy mix of gags à la Micallef and Commedia physical theatre. It was not always received with unadulterated delight. One afternoon in a school in Hackham West, performing to a group of Year 9s, was particularly brutal. My memory is of an all-out 50 minute battle which we comprehensively lost during which there was not a moment of silence from them. I remember giving thanks that there was no jiggy dance sans undergarments. I don't think my psyche could have survived.

Funerals and Circuses, Chutney

The highlight of my time in Magpie was *Funerals and Circuses*. It was written by Aboriginal playwright Roger Bennett with music by Paul Kelly, one of Australia's greatest singer/songwriters, who also acted in it. It dealt with racial tension in a small country town. The show started outside the theatre, continued in the foyer, which was dressed to look like a country pub, and the audience were subsequently herded outside the pub into the auditorium which was made up to look like the pub's exterior and the centre of town. I played two parts: a racist bouncer and a comic Swiss tourist with a non-functional motor scooter. Any of us who had any musical background at all were press-ganged into playing instruments and I found myself in a band as Paul Kelly's keyboard player. I still look back at that time with wonder. It was one of the hits of the Festival and toured to Melbourne and Canberra and was eventually my ticket out of Adelaide.

No less memorable was a tour of the Pitjantjatjara lands doing a show called *Chutney* for the Aboriginal communities in Pukatja, Indulkana, Amata, Pipalyatjara and Kaltjiri (Fregon). We camped out most of the time, and sometimes we even did our show outdoors if there wasn't a suitable building. It was a good show for the kids up there, part puppet show, part mask with music, a large crocodile, a monkey and not a lot of text.

We arrived in Kaltjiri (Fregon) about halfway through the tour. There was a shed available for us, but just outside the shed there was a concreted area that was exactly the right size, so we made the decision to do the show there. As we set up the entire community turned up to watch. We had kids sitting at the front, and then, a little way off, a row of cars and the adults of the community sitting on the bonnets, slightly distrustfully, withholding judgement, watching.

We were about twenty minutes into the show when a dogfight broke out a hundred yards off. We were unfazed. We were seasoned professionals, after all, and the show continued without losing a beat. The audience, however, were not as indifferent to its attractions. Within seconds, the entire community had disappeared to watch it and we were left playing to an empty space. This is the actor's nightmare. To be performing to no-one. Or worse, to be performing to an audience that obviously and demonstrably consider not watching you more interesting than watching you. There was a momentary hesitation this time. We looked at each other. Should we stop? Or what?

The author, proving he knows Paul Kelly to talk to. Funerals and Circuses, Magpie Theatre. (Photo: Lisa Tomasetti)

We kept on going and eventually the dogfight finished and most of the audience came back. It was, however, a very strange and somewhat humiliating experience. And it raised an interesting question.

Is what you're doing more interesting than a dogfight?

Because more often than not the answer is no. And then you need to ask yourself, 'Why not?'

Marat/Sade

I had been with Magpie for over two years. An intense period but such a positive one. I had been heckled by eight year olds, discovered Commedia, made to dance, introduced to mask work, and still not mastered a cartwheel. But most importantly I could now answer the question 'What do you do?' with the simple statement, 'I'm an actor', instead of the awkward shuffling and the muttered 'I do a bit of performing', which had been my stock standard response till then. I decided it was time to move on. The next step would be to try to get more work on the main stage.

John Gaden was leaving STCSA. The new Artistic Director was an unknown from New Zealand called Simon Phillips. Again, every actor in Adelaide lined up to audition and again I joined the throng.

I arrived too early for my audition and had to wait nervously in the foyer. Eventually a shoeless youth, dressed in black with one blue sock and one yellow, came to meet me. 'This must be the PA', I thought. It wasn't. Following this somewhat inauspicious beginning, I was cast in the show and it has been my good fortune to have worked with Simon several times over the years. His productions are intelligent and stylish and fun and the rehearsal room is always full of laughter. At the time of writing I'm working on *Shakespeare in Love* for the Melbourne Theatre Company. Directed by Simon Phillips. He is, as ever, dressed in black with differently hued socks and the rehearsal room is still a hilarious place to be.

This show was *Marat/Sade* or to give it its full title, *The Persecution and Assassination of Jean-Paul Marat as Performed by the Inmates of the Asylum of Charenton Under the Direction of the Marquis de Sade.* Which describes it perfectly. Around the end of the eighteenth century the public would regularly visit the asylum of Charenton to watch the patients put on plays. And de Sade was in fact a patient at the time and did actually direct plays there.

Not this one, obviously, it was written in 1963 by the German playwright Peter Weiss. Geoffrey Rush played Marat; the late and greatly lamented Bob Hornery, de Sade. I played one of the patients in the asylum.

It was a spectacular production. The audience, when they entered the theatre, was confronted with a huge circular steel cage with a bath in the centre. Everything white, including the cast's gowns. The set slowly filled with water over the course of the play, until, by the end, we were wading through a couple of inches of water. In white gowns.

This was the second time I came up against the No Underpants rule but this time I could see a logical reason for the rule. Once the water made contact with the white gowns, they became partly transparent and the sight of twentieth century underwear would have struck a false note. We all obeyed the rule this time, but the sight of ten actors doing backward rolls in a circle round the stage in an inch of water singing 'We want our revolution now' while desperately trying to preserve their modesty is probably burnt into the retinas of every person present.

My patient was a bishop who had lost his faith. At one point, the script required me to get worked up enough to start screaming out a sort of satanic prayer. I'm quickly overpowered by the guards, stripped and put into a shower. Every night as the moment came for me to lose it, I would try to work myself into a frenzy. It was never right. I would desperately try to dig deeper, to find something way down inside me that I could bring up. Or I would try to think sad thoughts, to get myself into a state of despair.

Neither of these things worked. It was a source of great frustration and I never managed to find the right emotional state. And it wasn't till some years later working on a play called *Things We Do For Love* that I realised what I'd been doing wrong. We'll get to that later. (See below p.123.)

I've only been naked on stage twice. This was the first time. I was happy to do it as a sort of rite of passage. 'I can do that', or more importantly, 'I've done that'. But I never approached the moment with anything but a slightly sinking feeling. The hardest time, however, was the first. In front of the cast and crew. After that, being naked in front of a group of people you don't necessarily know is far easier.

Fear of looking awkward is one the first things we need to confront if we want to go on stage. It prevents us from committing to the emotion or the action and we end up looking precisely the way we were fearing we would.

Actors tend to manage this by wearing a cloak of 'Je m'en foutisme'. From the French, 'Je m'en fous', I don't give a fuck. I've seen actors identified as such in the street, merely because of their manner. Their je m'en foutisme.

Je m'en foutisme makes it possible for me to wear a ridiculously small costume, to roll around on the floor screaming about my mother, to take my clothes off and do the macarena. And to do these things without a second thought. Moreover, because I am carrying out these actions without embarrassment and also with total commitment, I achieve a kind of dignity. Paradoxically, the more I willingly abandon my ego and the more vulnerable I make myself, the more dignity I accrue.

So don't worry about your ego, it just gets in the way of the moment.

Just tell yourself – Je m'en fous.

Simon loved and loves actors, he loves rehearsal rooms and he loves giving notes. And if you are in the mood, it's enormous fun. Sitting around with the cast after a show, talking about the play you've all just done, with a drink in your hand, is not work, it's a party.

But if you have an early start it can be taxing. And there are usually always some actors who just want to get their notes, get home and go to bed. And generally, notes sessions aren't little parties, they're part of the work.

Here is how to take a note from a director:

> DIRECTOR: Francis, when you come on with the bicycle, could you wheel it downstage a little further before you start screaming?

FRANCIS: Yes. *(Writes it down.)*
    The end.

Your fellow actors will be grateful.

Notes, like direction, are just a means of improving the performance. They're not a criticism. You're very lucky someone is watching you and trying to make you and the production look better.

I once worked on a show with an actor who found it very difficult to take notes. Every time the director gave him one, he would explain why he couldn't do it or suggest that the problem was one of the other actors. The director was very patient with him, but I remember thinking at the time, 'He's never going to cast you in anything again.'

And I was right.

Don't be that actor. Take the note. It's for your own benefit.

School for Scandal

It's a truism that it's hard to break into the acting world. You can't get work if you haven't got an agent and you can't get an agent without any work to show them. Theatre directors do often hold auditions, but equally, and naturally, they sometimes prefer to cast actors they know and have worked with and who they think are right for the part. It saves time. They have a stable of actors, and the same faces show up in their plays again and again. Annoying if you're not part of the in crowd. Some sort of stability if you are.

Now I had left Magpie, I became, in a small way, part of Simon Phillips' Adelaide stable and he cast me in *School for Scandal*, Sheridan's Restoration comedy about gossip. I played Sir Benjamin Backbite, one of the coterie that gathers regularly to bitch about anyone not in the room. On the first day of rehearsals, Simon suggested my character have a speech impediment. That he be unable to say the letter 'r' correctly. Like the late Terry Thomas. YouTube him if you don't know who that is.

It's very unusual for a director to prescribe a performance like that on the first day of rehearsals. Or indeed on any day. Overwhelmingly, character is something that the actor needs to come to by themselves. However, I was young and amenable and in need of guidance and I accepted the instruction without a second thought. I'm very glad I did, as it fitted the character beautifully. A more experienced actor might not have taken it so well. As we shall see.

Because, amazingly, I'm not the first to be put in this exact position.

One of my favourite acting books is *About Acting* by Peter Barkworth, an English actor and acting teacher. It's a collection of useful acting tips. It is, in part, the inspiration for this book.

Peter describes a production of *School for Scandal* directed by theatre great John Gielgud where he was playing … Sir Benjamin

Backbite. And on the first day of rehearsals Gielgud suggested he have exactly the same impediment that Simon suggested to me. An extraordinary coincidence. Barkworth was not quite so keen on the idea and, probably because of this, the motif never worked. I was grateful for the offer and that's why it worked for me.

During rehearsals, Gielgud gave Barkworth many more ideas for his performance, up to and including balancing a cane on the tip of his chin. And Barkworth found himself in a very awkward position. Physically and metaphorically.

The question of what you do when a director gives you a direction you don't agree with is a tricky one. Theatre in Australia is a benevolent dictatorship with the director at the top. It's their show. They point the designer in the direction they want, they approve costume well before the rehearsals start, they dictate the blocking. If a director says jump, you generally say 'Is this high enough?'

And, let's face it, often the director is the best placed to make decisions. They're the ones watching from the outside and they're the ones that have the whole production in mind, not just one performance. More often than not, they're right.

However, there is a little leeway. There are several factors at play: your relationship with the director; the way they work; how determined you are to do it your way; even, sadly, your seniority in the cast and/or profession. Moreover, a director will not want to make you do something against your will – there's nothing worse than trying to direct a grumpy actor and so they will often back off if you make a strong case. However, you can't always be arguing. *If a director is asking you to do something that you don't think will work, at least give it a go. Properly. With commitment.* Then, if it doesn't work, you've shown you gave it the proverbial red hot and you can discuss alternatives.

In Peter Barkworth's case, he eventually raised the issue with another one of the actors who told him not to be so obedient. That Gielgud was just throwing ideas out and they weren't to be taken as gospel. And that is quite common too. I vividly remember, during rehearsals for *The Tempest*, John Gaden producing a tray and a bottle and suggesting I carry it on with me. I was rigid with fear at the time.

The author and Celia de Burgh trying to ignore the lack of furniture. School for Scandal, STC(SA). (Photo: David Wilson)

I didn't or couldn't incorporate them in the scene and John, wisely, didn't push it.

I have known actors who say 'Yes' to a note, write it down very carefully and then completely ignore it. Often directors will give the same note two or three times and if it's not taken up they will assume that the actor either can't or won't carry it out and drop the issue.

I couldn't possibly recommend it as a *modus operandi*, but I may or may not have used it myself upon occasion.

I suppose the thing to take away here is that **theatre is a collaborative process and no one person – the director, writer or actor – is going to get their way 100 per cent of the time.** No-one completely achieves their vision, it's always leavened by someone else's contribution. Which makes it frustrating and also wonderful.

My character wouldn't do that. This is the other side of the coin. When perhaps it's not the director who's the problem. It's just the actor being a pain. I will never forget rehearsals for a certain show being brought to a standstill by one actor's refusal to change her entrance. Apparently her character 'wouldn't do that'. Slightly irritating as we were re-rehearsing a show for a different venue and the original entrance didn't exist anymore.

After what seemed like an hour of discussion, the actor in question grumpily agreed to try it. We restarted rehearsals.

Later, when we eventually found ourselves back in the first venue, the director said, 'Thanks, X, you can go back to the original entrance now.' 'No', came the response. 'I like it this way.'

Collapse of stout party. That's a quote from *Punch*, not a description of any of the actors involved.

Nine times out of ten, if you find yourself saying 'but my character wouldn't do that', you've slightly lost the plot. It's your job as an actor to justify the action. If the director wants you to sit down before speaking, then there are surely a dozen motivations you can find to sit. That's what an actor does, surely: they find motivation for their actions and words. It's the job description.

Generally it comes down to a rather limited view of character. **A human being is a very complex thing, and if you think you completely understand all aspects of your character then you might have to think again.** I can hold completely opposing views quite easily, depending on the circumstances, or I can hold one view in one situation and then turn on a dime and believe the opposite, or I can say one thing and believe it utterly, but do something that completely contradicts what I've said and not feel like a hypocrite. And this sort of behaviour is not remarkable, people act like this *all the time*.

Perhaps instead of thinking that your character wouldn't do something, it might be a better attitude to give it a go and be thankful for the chance to investigate the contradictory and complex nature of the person you're playing.

At the end of the day, it's not Shakespeare. It probably won't affect the artistic purity of the piece if you speak the line regretfully instead of defiantly for instance, it's just a different slant on things.

And even if it *is* Shakespeare, quite often it's not.

As it were.

Of course, sometimes the director *is* wrong. Very wrong. And then you're back to square one.

This was the only time Simon ever imposed something on me. He's not that sort of director. And while I was grateful for it at the time, I also appreciated his usual *modus operandi* which was to trust that he had cast the right person and to let them do their job. They do say that direction is 90 per cent casting. That if you've got the right actor, then a lot of your work is done for you. And that's generally what Simon did. He would only step in if things were going off the rails.

It's easy to spot an inexperienced director: they tend to want you to perform it the way they see it in their head. And the rehearsal process tends to involve them telling you what to do. I worked with a director who was so determined that what you did tallied with what he had in his head that he would give line readings for every single line. I saw several performances completely demolished by this process. The actor always ended up trying to copy him, which is death.

Nowadays I really value the director who feels secure enough to look at what the actor brings and work with that.

Rehearsals for *School for Scandal* were fun. I had worked out Sir Benjamin's walk quite early on – it was a sort of glide, almost like a dancer – and I was enjoying myself greatly. The production was quite different from the usual Restoration comedy production. There was no set. No tables, no chairs, no chaise longue on which to recline as we delivered our biting repartee. Instead, six mirrors of increasing size, that could reflect or be seen through, depending on the lights, and six servants, also of increasing size, whose only job was to move the mirrors about to create the environment.

As for the actors, the idea was that our sinuous moves, round about each other, would complement the sinuosity of the language as we vilified absent characters and tried to outdo those present. It was an interesting and potentially wonderful idea, but I'm not sure that we quite achieved it. Often rehearsals would begin with trying to remember the blocking of the rehearsal before and by the time we'd recreated it, we only had a few minutes left to build on it. *Ad infinitum*.

And it's tricky when you don't really know your fellow cast members. As Celia de Burgh, who was playing Lady Sneerwell, said when we were about to go into the theatre, 'We know each other well enough now to start rehearsals.' It was a production an ensemble would have gone to town on. We became an ensemble too late.

The play was extremely funny, if extremely wordy. And that is the nature of Restoration comedy – you need a lot of breath control to manage the line to its end, to keep the energy up all the way through. Not easy for Australians. That sort of controlled, energetic speech doesn't come naturally to us at all.

I still remember one of my lines. I'm talking about the rumour surrounding Miss Nicely and her footman. Mrs Candour has just expressed doubts about its truth because Miss Nicely is usually so quiet.

'O Lud! Ma'am that's the very reason t'was believed at once. She has always been so cautious and so reserved that everybody was sure there was some reason for it at bottom.'

Amusing in context, slightly baffling here.

Towards the end of the rehearsal process, searching for something new, I changed the word 'reserved' to the French 'réservée'. Not the most brilliant comic invention ever, but it got a big laugh from the cast. So I kept it in.

Opening night arrived, off we went, the laughs came freely, and all was well. But when I came to the 'réservée' line, not a sausage. It was as though I had broken wind in public or praised Hitler. Or done stand-up at a Christmas party for a group of builders. And for the rest of the season, until I went back to the original, I never got even the smallest titter.

I realise now that it was a rehearsal joke, based on an awareness of the original line. Which the audience don't have. There is nothing amusing about someone using a French word in conversation. It's not going to provoke laughter. It's only funny if you know what the script actually is and you've done the scene over and over again and all the humour has been leached out of it and then, thank God, someone does something different and then suddenly it's hilarious again.

These sorts of laughs often happen in the dreaded third week of rehearsals, when things are at their bleakest. Our characters don't work, there's no energy, the scenes feel flat and lifeless and we just can't see the light at the end of the tunnel. And we grasp at straws and laugh at anything new.

But it's important to tell yourself it's all going to be fine and to go on just trusting the script. And if you can just wait until the first preview, all is revealed. And then you finally see the show from an audience's point of view after working inside it for so long and you realise that the line you thought was hilarious is not and the line that you never had much time for stops the show.

So beware the rehearsal laugh – the chances are it won't translate to an audience.

Così

Another Simon Phillips production, Louis Nowra's *Così*. Another play about patients in a mental hospital putting on a play but more contemporary this time. I played the social worker. A minor character. Just three small scenes. No matter, no small parts, just small actors. Not true actually, some parts are tiny. Like this one.

At about this time I found myself at a design workshop for high school students given by designer Mary Moore. A lot of it is lost in time but I do vividly remember her putting a large ball and a brightly coloured towel down on the floor. 'Where are we?' And the answer was obviously on the beach. A towel and a scented candle and a book took us into the bathroom, and a towel, deodorant and bottle of water put us in the changing room at the gym.

It was a revelation for me. **The ability of a very small object to do a lot of work.**

Back at rehearsals, I was determined to make something of my cameo. After much thought, I put bicycle clips on my trousers. And after even more thought I entered in my second scene wiping my hands on a handkerchief. Brilliant. I was now a social worker who rode his bicycle to work. I was a slightly absent-minded social worker, who forgot to remove his bicycle clips, and I had no sense of style. I was a social worker who had to deal with maintenance issues (perhaps funding was scarce) and I was a social worker with a loose relationship to hygiene as I was choosing to wipe the dirt off my hands with the thing I usually applied to my nose, instead of using soap and water.

Not the most brilliant ideas ever, but I did give the character a life without adding to my few lines, and with just a couple of very small touches.

The power of the prop to suggest a world. What does answering the door with a tea-towel mean? Or a newspaper? Or a paintbrush? What am I saying if I come on stage with a yoga mat? Or a pair of binoculars? Or a very small plastic bag, tied at the top?

A prop can be a two-edged sword, however. Especially the principal prop in that possibly imaginary play *Eduardo and the Two-Edged Sword*.

Props can really help things. Dialogue while carrying out a task tends to become more natural. The words come out more easily, because we're focused on something else. Years later, shooting the family drama, *Winners and Losers*, it was amazing how easy it was to casually toss off the line 'Who wants a cuppa then?' while you were picking up the kettle and moving to the sink.

But make sure you're really using the prop. If you're doing the washing up, then make sure you wash up. One of your objectives here is cleaning dishes – you must actually get those dishes cleaned. There's nothing that takes the reality out of a scene more than seeing someone dick around with crockery and soapy water. With no purpose.

And for God's sake, ***if you're walking down the street holding a take-away coffee then make sure that it's full of water.*** There's nothing that undermines the suspension of disbelief like an actor pretending to drink from a cup that is obviously empty. And if you can get the art department to give you something hot to drink, even better.

Similarly with heavier things. If you're carrying a suitcase make sure it's got something heavy in it, so you don't have to 'act' the weight.

Years later, during Shaun Micallef's satirical TV show *Mad as Hell*, I had to load sacks of wheat onto a truck. They weren't heavy at all so I was endowing them with weight, puffing and straining and committing to the act of lifting heavy sacks like a heavy sack maestro. When the scene was aired, I realised that the actor taking the sacks from me was just picking them up and tossing them into the truck as if they were light as a feather, which they were. And I looked like an idiot. Which wouldn't have happened if the sacks had been weighted.

So use props properly. As it were.

But don't forget, as well as the props you use, there are also the props you don't. You just carry them. The tea-towel, the wet umbrella, the suitcase. They're more like badges. They help define your character. Don't forget these. They can be very helpful.

The Club

I was slowly starting to get more work. And it's usually the case that work begets work. I was cast in David Williamson's *The Club*, one of the great Australian plays and almost idiot-proof. It's hard to put it on and for it not to work. I played Ted, the club president. David Field played the coach, Syd Brisbane the captain of the team, and Don Barker, a fixture of Adelaide's theatre scene, stole the show as the ex-president who gets unknowingly stoned. I remember Don telling me that many of his contemporaries had either died or left the industry and that he was now one of the few actors of his age in Adelaide. 'Now I get all the jobs.'

I resolved to outlive all of my peers too.

But slightly sinister resolutions aside, **the only common denominator in actors with career longevity is persistence.** They never give up. Often actors get tired of the lifestyle, the irregularity and insecurity of work and find something else to do. And there's absolutely nothing wrong with that decision – if you haven't had any work for a significant period of time, then you do need to assess where you are and if you're doing the right thing. But if you want to still be an actor when you're 60, you need to keep doing it until you get there.

The Club opened in Adelaide and toured, on and off, for six months.

It was directed by Rosalba Clemente. Rosalba had an interesting way of directing. We would run through a scene and then she would systematically take each of us aside and give us notes privately. Then we would run it again. You never knew what your fellow actors were going to do. As in life, I suppose.

I remember having problems with my character. I just couldn't comprehend the man. I could focus on elements of his personality but I couldn't bring them all together and turn them into one easily assimilable thing. I couldn't *know* him. It was very frustrating.

One night at home, after rehearsals, I went outside to experiment with Ted's physicality. I imagined him outside too, around a barbecue, holding forth, with a beer in one hand and a cigarette in the other. And suddenly a physical shape came to me. I stuck my bottom out and my stomach out in the other direction. It gave me a slightly pugnacious aspect and forced me to waddle rather than walk. More importantly, it felt right. It was easy to do. It was organic, even though to some extent it was artificially created. And I had the character.

The physical stance and walk became the platform for everything else, and I stopped worrying about trying to understand who the character was. **Because, of course, you can't ever fully comprehend a character.** You can't hold all the complexity and variety of one human being in your hand and say 'That's who it is'. But having one solid point, the walk, allowed me to proceed and develop him and stopped me worrying about not being able to define him.

There's a story Dustin Hoffman tells about the filming of *Rain Man*. He was finding it impossible to get the character of Raymond, an autistic savant. He couldn't work out what was going on in Raymond's head. He was completely lost and frustrated. So much so, in fact, that he was about to pull out of the film. Finally, one day, Hoffman and Tom Cruise, playing his brother, were shooting a driving scene. Just the two of them in the car, the camera fixed to the window and Barry Levinson, the director, at the other end of a walkie-talkie. They finished the scene and Barry told them to drive back to the base and just improvise on the way back. So they did. Or rather Cruise did. Hoffman didn't have the character and, however hard he tried, he couldn't find a way to contribute. He just couldn't respond.

They got back to where Levinson was waiting and before Hoffman could say anything, Levinson jumped in, 'Have a look at the footage.' And when Hoffman did, he saw he'd finally cracked it. He'd only said one word the whole time. 'Yes.' Quite testily. As he couldn't think of anything else to say. But that 'yes' gave him the character. It was the 'yes' of a man who didn't know what to say. Who couldn't interact. Which was actually pure Hoffman. And that one word became something solid to stand on and the character was born.

There are no rules here. It's whatever gets you from A to B.

The author, relating a recent fishing expedition to David Field in The Club, *STC(SA). (Photo: Eric Algra)*

It's a tricky concept, character. In one sense it doesn't exist. In *Dimensions of Acting*, the sagacious Terence Crawford suggests that perhaps 'the illusion of "character" is an audience's privilege'. That what they see from the outside is very different from what is happening inside the actor. Which is just the process of 'being' in the circumstances. And even if the actor is doing nothing specific to create a character, just the act of being and reacting is perceived as character by the audience. So perhaps there's no need to stress about 'transforming' – walks or noses or whatever. Just absorb the given circumstances and be in the moment. And that's the character.

And again, some actors are transformational by nature. They present very different parts of themselves according to the role, and they appear to be different people. Some don't seem to change at all. Often they're the ones playing the leads. Cary Grant was Cary Grant in every single film he ever did.

But that doesn't mean that the transformational character actors are doing better character work; it depends on the part and on the individual actor. Much later, when I played Brian Gross in *Winners and Losers*, I didn't feel much need to alter anything much and certainly not my walk. There were things I concentrated on internally – Brian's attitude to the world for example, and not sounding too English, as I do normally, but I didn't really need to sculpt him from outside.

But sometimes there is quite a distance from the character and our day-to-day selves. Either in time: we may be playing a Shakespearean monarch; or in age; or in simply in who we are. In *The Club*, I felt Ted was quite different from me in many respects. And that I needed to transform myself a bit. Sometimes we do need to sculpt ourselves a little. And often in these situations, for me, it's the walk. Especially, as I've said, if the distance between the character and myself is great. If I can work out how the character walks, then I'm okay. Apparently Alec Guinness was the same, so I'm in good company. For Laurence Olivier, they say, it was the nose. But then the guy always was weird. Whatever gets you through the night.

You've got to be careful though, as you won't be the first person to give their character a limp, or a lisp. Just as I wasn't the first to give Sir Benjamin Backbite a soft 'r'. But if it fits, it fits. In the 1981 TV version of *Brideshead Revisited*, the actor Nickolas Grace gives his character Anthony Blanche both a stammer *and* soft 'r'. The stammer is indicated in the novel but the 'r' is not. It could have been a disaster, but it wasn't. It's outrageous and brilliant. I've spent my life waiting for a part where I can copy that, but sadly among the policemen, lawyers and priests that the Australian TV industry has asked me to play over the years, I have never found a character that could cope with such extravagant vocal stylings. I live in hope.

Sometimes I start with what the character isn't. That doesn't feel right, I won't do that anymore. With Brian Gross it was removing any hint of Englishness. A few years ago, doing Neil Simon's *The Odd Couple*, Peter Houghton, the director, asked me to stop pointing so much. And I was doing a lot of pointing. I don't know why. But he was right, it was all a bit much. It didn't really fit with Oscar Madison, the character I was playing. So I stopped. And I found a tiny but important element of Oscar's character. He doesn't point much.

Sometimes it's good to start with what to leave out.

As I've said before, there are no rules here. Every situation is different – what works for Williamson won't necessarily work for Shakespeare and everyone's approach is unique.

Towards the end of the play Ted is forced to resign. He has one last speech, all alone in the middle of the stage and then leaves, beaten but unbowed. One night, during the tour, on stage in Geraldton, I realised I had forgotten the character's glasses. This unsettled me and I couldn't get into my speech. I just found myself saying the words and when I made my exit, I couldn't access the feelings I usually felt when I left. I was annoyed. It was Ted's final statement and not to nail it like that was most unsatisfactory.

Rosalba was in that night. 'You were very vulnerable during that speech,' she said. 'It really worked.'

We get into a routine, during a run. We become comfortable. But it's good to get pushed outside our comfort zone. That's when we really become alive and in the moment. John Gielgud used to put a small pebble in his shoe whenever he was filming. To keep himself on edge. Outside his comfort zone. **Paradoxically, it's sometimes the moments when we feel least in control of the work, that we are most true to the situation.**

Another night on stage during the run I forgot a line. There was an awkward pause, the line just wouldn't come. The pause lengthened. Someone else said something, I remembered the line, blurted it out and we continued on. But I couldn't get back into the play. Every subsequent line felt fake, I was just skating on the surface. And then I started to obsess about my inability to get back into it. And I never did get back into it that night. I was in hell until the curtain call. It was my worst night in the theatre ever. So far. Touch wood.

Everyone loses lines occasionally. It's an occupational hazard, like a beekeeper being stung or a carpenter hitting himself on the thumb.

I quite frequently find myself on stage, suddenly realising I have no idea what my next line is. And I don't think I'm alone in having this experience.

The thing to do is to relax and trust that the line will be there. And it will. If you relax. If you stress about it, then you will be too concerned about the possibility of not knowing the line when it comes up to have any space in your head for the line to appear. And after all, in real life, we never know exactly what we are going to say next either, so tell yourself that you're having a moment of utter truth. You are 'in the moment'. You couldn't be more present. And you'll be fine.

Nowadays, I can recognise that feeling of blankness and know from experience that the line is there. And that if I relax and breathe it will appear. But it took me a while to get there.

But when you do eventually and inevitably lose that line, the thing to keep in mind is that **there is only one person to whom the lost line matters and that's you.** The audience have moved on, if they even realised anything was amiss, as have the cast – they've got better things to think about. And after the show, no-one except you will even remember anything about it. So why are you obsessing?

Easy to say. Not so easy to put into practice. It's really only time that helps with this one.

The lovely thing about the State Theatre Company at that time was that everything was in the same place. The rehearsal rooms, the wardrobe department, the workshop, the admin staff, the theatre and the bar. And this created a very strong sense of community about the place. Generally.

One night after we came down (and plays never finish, they come down. Although in my experience, that's not always what happens. Sometimes they fall down. And sometimes you have to drag them up the hill. I digress.) One night after we came down, I entered the bar to find a group of admin staff laughing at something the new Artistic Director of the company had drawn on a piece of paper.

'Look at this', someone said. 'It's a picture of your feet.' And it was. It was a crudely drawn picture of two feet with movement lines around them to indicate movement. 'That's you', the AD said. 'You've got twitchy feet. You never stand still.' I had a good relationship with the Artistic Director, so I wasn't overly upset; however, it was slightly confronting to have my work critiqued so publicly. But my feet did stop twitching.

And now it's the first thing I say to young actors if they come to me for coaching. **Keep still.** There's usually an enormous amount of energy coming out of the student and instead of it being directed into what they are thinking about and how that will be expressed, it comes out in the body. In little shuffles, forward and back, from one foot to the other. It distracts from the rest of the performance. I occasionally resort to putting a couple of old exercise books on the students' feet to keep them stationary. The students, that is. The books are already stationery. It's a simple thing but it makes such a difference. ***Just plant your feet and don't move them unless you want to go somewhere.***

Then there's the question of pacing. 'I thought I might pace up and down?' And I always discourage it. We only move because we want to go somewhere. ***We never really move purposelessly***. We might move because we want to do something or go somewhere and then stop when we realise that the action won't accomplish what we want, or there isn't anywhere to go, but we've always got an end in mind.

And if I'm agitated I might go and pick something up and then put it down and go to sit down to wait and then stand up to look out of the window and change my mind and sit down again and it may look purposeless, but it's not, it's very purposeful. Many purposes. ***So if you are going to move, make sure it's to go somewhere or do something.***

Accidental Death of an Anarchist

One last job for the State Theatre Company. I was cast in Dario Fo's *Accidental Death of an Anarchist* directed by Robyn Archer and with comedian Mick Molloy in the lead. *Accidental Death of an Anarchist* is based on the real-life death of an Italian anarchist at police hands, after he was framed for the bombing of a bank. A strange character known only as the Madman infiltrates the police station where the anarchist died and persuades the police that he is a judge reopening the enquiry into the anarchist's death. This was Mick's first stage role and he did an excellent job. Robyn cast Indigenous journalist Michelle Tuahini as the journalist Feletti and gave Mick a speech about Aboriginals continuing to die in custody, despite a Royal Commission some years earlier. Audiences were irritated.

'I don't need a lecture about Aboriginal deaths in custody.'

'Oh, really?'

I was cast as an unnamed Constable, comedian Vince Sorrenti played Inspector Pisani and Jo Spano was the Superintendent. It was clever casting. Jo was the shortest in the cast but the highest in rank, Vince was taller than him but subordinate to him, and as the lowly Constable I was taller still.

Which brings me to the topic of what I call small-s status. A huge subject and one which deserves its own heading. And indeed, a new page.

Status

We all know what social status is. If you're a Supreme Court judge with two houses, a flat in Paris, children at private schools and membership of the Melbourne Club and the Melbourne Cricket Ground, then I'm surprised that you're reading this book. And a little pleased. But what's more, you have a high social status. Capital-S Status. Well done. The small-s status I'm referring to is something less enduring. It could be described as who has the upper hand in the situation. Who is top, or bottom, of the heap at the moment.

This sort of status is entirely dependent on context. The Supreme Court judge has a high social status wherever he/she goes or whatever happens. Not so with small-s status. If I am teaching students, I have a high small-s status because I am the teacher and the students are lowly worms, scrabbling for the crumbs of learning that drop from my mouth. To mix metaphors. But if one of the students appears to know more than I do about the subject, and starts arguing with me, my status will drop and theirs will rise. And if we finish up and go for a drink at some nightclub where young beautiful people congregate to drink and dance and Instagram each other, then I, being over 50 years old, am just a creepy old man hanging round young people and my status plummets. Context is all. The Supreme Court judge is in the same room as a respected medical specialist. Who has the higher small-s status? Well, if they're in the doctor's surgery because the judge has an embarrassing skin condition, the doctor has the higher status, but if the room in question is the judge's courtroom and the doctor is having to explain why they have confronting photographs or the instructions for making bombs on their laptop, then it's obviously the judge whose status is higher.

This idea of status is important for two reasons. First, it's a useful bit of vocabulary when you're rehearsing: 'The character needs to be more high status', or 'The character needs to start out low status and then gain status throughout the scene' and so on. It's a very handy lens that allows us to look at a scene in a different way. But, secondly, it's also important because this is how people interact, and, if we as actors need to know anything, it's what motivates and drives people to do and say what they say and do. So anything that can help us understand the interactions of people is worth going into in greater depth.

And it's quite possible to view any human interaction as a jostling or bargaining for status. Sometimes agreed upon, sometimes fought for.

Males especially, since their egos are often somewhat more brittle than female egos, are constantly trying to achieve high status vis-à-vis each other. *The Footy Show* was a TV show devoted to Australian Rules Football, featuring past and present players. This televisual celebration of the great Australian game was an hour of alpha males each trying to achieve a higher status than the rest of the panel, either by pumping themselves up or, more typically, by bringing someone else down. It was not a very edifying spectacle but it is a good example of the status negotiations that can occur when males come into contact with each other.

Two men are walking down the street towards each other on a collision course. They notice each other. Immediately a game of chicken begins and the one who eventually steps aside has their status lowered.

Men fight these status battles constantly. Often without knowing. If two men are walking towards a lift or a doorway, one will often indicate to the other to go through first. This is on the surface a kind gesture but in actual fact it's checkmate in a little status game. If you let someone go first, you are actually seizing high status. You are saying, 'This is my door and I'm going to let you go first.' It's taking control of who moves when, even though it's seemingly using that power benevolently. Whenever it happens to me I think 'Well, bugger you' as I go through. Or words to that effect. And it is checkmate because there is really no way not to lose status. Either you go through or you don't. If you go through, you lose status. The only other alternative is to try to get the other to go first and then you're opening yourself up to further status loss because the first person will inevitably repeat his initial 'You first', and then you're locked into a 'No, you', 'No you' little war. ***And if you tell someone to do something and they don't, then your status instantly drops*** and continues to drop until one of you reluctantly accepts the loss of status and goes through.

I am unsure whether women play these sorts of games. Men tend to be slightly cruder when it comes to status. And at the risk of making wild and unsubstantiated generalisations, it is often the case that women, because they tend to be socialised at an earlier age than men, understand these things better and play status games at a slightly more sophisticated level. 'That's a nice top. I had one like that.'

You can also play low status games. Students are especially good at this.

'I'm going to fail this exam.'

'No you're not, you're really good at French.'

'But I haven't done any revision.'

'It doesn't matter, at least you understand it. I just can't do it full stop.'

And the game is a low status one. Who is the laziest and most stupid student in the class.

The rules of the game can change in an instant too. I show someone something on my iPhone 8. They show me how it's better on an iPhone X. Person three has an iPhone Hasn't-been-released-yet that they got from a friend in Silicon Valley and we're in a full-on status battle of who is the more electronically sophisticated. Person four pulls out their Nokia.

'I don't have time for social media, I really just use this for calls.'

And the game of who is the most technologically advanced has suddenly turned into a game of who has the purest and most uncluttered life, and we've all just had the rug pulled out from under our feet.

It's worth noting too we can have a status relationship with our environment. We are high status to our living rooms or kitchens for example. We know where everything is and we treat objects with familiarity. An operating theatre where we are the patient, or an audition room or a forest at midnight, these are all places that have high status, or rather we have low status to them. Worth thinking about when you are making your entrance.

So how do we achieve high status on stage? Well, obviously if we think high status, we will radiate high status. The body obeys the mind, so if we have really understood exactly who the character is then we will move about on stage in a way that expresses our high status at that moment. But we can help ourselves here. As I've noted above, just as the body obeys the mind, so the mind responds to physical cues from the body. So if we want to achieve high status it's good to know what that looks like physically.

When I teach status to students, I generally get two volunteers up at this stage. I tell one just to stay still and the other to fiddle with their hair, scratch their nose, to find whatever reasons they can to simply touch their face. We watch them for a few seconds and it is obvious to everyone that the stiller one has higher status, even though the only difference between the two is physical.

High status characters are generally still. Lower status characters fidget. Useful information. You might be trying to play a high status character but you notice you're shuffling, or twitching a little. If you just make a physical adjustment, you will start to look, and therefore also feel, more high status.

Actors generally have a status speciality, even if they don't know it. They are better at low status characters or happier playing high. I once directed a student who had a large and imposing physique. He was magnificent at characters with gravitas. High status characters. He would plant himself and deliver. However his physical presence made it very hard for him to play low status. He couldn't fidget. Eventually, by accident, I made him so unsure of himself that when he came to do the scene he was so much at sea that he became a low status human and he gave a very good low status performance. But that's not the way to direct. Some directors will use the actor's own insecurities to make them actually cry. I call that psychological abuse, not directing.

So status. Very useful. Read Keith Johnstone's book *Impro*.

It's a beautiful book about being a creative human, not just about performing. And the stuff about status is fascinating.

Another thought. Some actors would rather play high status than low. I see a lot of actor's showreels that consist of scenes where tough guys point guns at people or have guns pointed at them, and don't seem at all worried by the situation. In a very high status way. But high status is boring if it's overused. A series of events is only interesting if they affect the characters. And it's low status characters that generally are the most affected by things happening to them. High status characters are too cool. Hence their attraction. But the more things and events affect you, the more engaging the story.

And what is more significant than having a gun poked in your face? If you don't show yourself affected by it, what's the point? If you're terrified by the gun, but yet you somehow manage to conquer those fears, then you've got a story.

Howard Fine tells a story about working on a scene. A man and a woman go through a break-up. It's not really firing. He asks the male actor what's going on for him and the man says he doesn't think he's really in love with the girl. Which is strictly his right to do as the one playing the character. Fine's response is – why are we doing the scene then? If the break-up doesn't matter, then the scene doesn't either. Or to put it another way, it's not interesting if the events don't affect the characters. He suggests that as a general rule you should make the stakes as high as possible. Otherwise the scene is boring. If you get a letter saying your electricity is about to be cut off, then let it really matter. If it's just a minor irritation, then what's the point of it happening?

So if you find yourself constantly being cast in low status roles, enjoy it. They are the most interesting ones anyway. That's not to say high status characters aren't interesting. But generally only if their status is challenged. And if the actor lets the character be affected by what's happening.

So that's status. Useful.

Back to *Accidental Death of an Anarchist*. While we were on stage at the Playhouse, Stephen Berkoff, the enfant terrible of the English theatre, was doing a show in The Space next door. We shared a green room. He was a commanding presence, but pleasant enough. I remember we played pool with him during intervals.

The Constable, my role in *Accidental Death*, is not a large part. He has a line every once in a while, but he's on stage for just about the whole play. For most of the time, I found myself standing upstage, in a corner, with pages of dialogue before my next line, the triangle player in the Fo orchestra and I have to confess my attention did occasionally wander. One matinee, I noticed how few people there were in the audience.

'I bet I could count them', I thought. And started to.

I'd got to about twenty or so when I saw Stephen Berkoff. Sitting by himself near the back. And he wasn't even watching. He had his head turned round as though he was counting the audience himself. Which he may well have been. As far as I remember, we weren't setting the world on fire that afternoon. But it was extremely disconcerting and I stopped counting and was on my best behaviour after that.

I don't know that I have to say this. But I will. **Don't count the audience.**

Moving

It was 1993 and I had been working as an actor for five years. It seems a lot longer in retrospect. Partly I suspect because my learning curve had been so huge. I had done a lot of theatre but hardly any TV. There was one memorable night, playing Policeman Three on *The New Adventures of Black Beauty*. I had one scene and one line.

We filmed in Belair National Park. It was a night shoot and raining heavily. I found myself standing in the rain at 2:00 a.m., dressed as a constable from the 1920s, holding a lantern powered by an electrical cable which snaked up my sleeve, down my shirt, down my trousers, across several puddles and was connected to a small generator while two horses drawing a stagecoach thundered down a small track towards me. And they say it's not a glamorous profession. But that was about it as much as the South Australian film industry offered. And there was no TV industry at all. If I wanted to move on to roles where I had more lines than just 'Halt!', and less chance of death by electrocution, I had to move.

I discussed this with Shaun Micallef, who was now working as a solicitor. We decided we would move to Melbourne together. We would become stars. The city would fall at our feet. Preparations were made. I had a farewell party, people gave me presents, Shaun booked a double room in a hotel in Little Bourke Street as a launching pad and off we went. People came to the train and waved us off with banners. Well, they didn't, but I did make a big fuss about saying goodbye and people rightly assumed that I wouldn't be back.

We arrived, sat in our hotel room and wondered what to do. We mooched about Melbourne, annoyed each other, and managed seven and a half minutes of stand-up each. I ran out of money, no-one fell at our feet and after a week we gave up and decided to catch the train home. I packed my not inconsiderable amount of luggage and suggested we catch a taxi to the station. Shaun wanted to walk. Stalemate.

As I staggered down Swanston Street, carrying approximately one hundred bags and suitcases, leaving the dreams of making it lying shattered in pieces behind me and trying not to drop my guitar, a tall, imposing looking man came towards me. Am I racist if I mention he was African American? Dreadlocks, sunglasses, street cred oozing from every pore. He veered to avoid me, stopped, considered me and then delivered his verdict. 'Faggot.'

And moved on.

The end of a wonderful week.

Back in Adelaide, bloodied but unbowed, I sheephishly said hello to those that I had farewelled for ever and considered my next move. A few months later, I did actually manage to make the move. Luck was on my side. A phone call got me a job as an understudy on an outdoor production of *Twelfth Night*. Steven Gration's brother had a spare room. I had two months undemanding work while I settled into Melbourne. And I was on my way.

I arrived in Melbourne and was at work immediately. Being an understudy is a strange job. There's half an hour of vague stress while you wait for the actors you are understudying to arrive, but once they do, you're basically off duty.

And I did eventually go on. As a non-speaking monk. Tiny steps. My job was to bring a torch, soaking in kerosene in a bucket, on stage, stick the torch in the ground, light it, pick up the bucket and leave. Simple. The cigarette lighter they gave me to use was of a sort guaranteed never to go out even in the fiercest wind. You actually had to close the lid to stop the flame. What could possibly go wrong?

I made my first appearance on a Melbourne stage. Or Melbourne grass. I entered, stuck the torch in the ground and lit it, but somehow, instead of closing the lighter's lid and putting it into my pocket, I didn't close it, and dropped it into the bucket. I waited for my cue to exit. The audience started laughing. Which was odd, as the moment wasn't supposed to be comic at all. I glanced down and noticed that the kerosene in the bucket had caught on fire.

'I'm not picking that thing up', I thought to myself and left, to even greater gales of laughter. Stage management raced on stage, removed the now fiercely blazing object and the play went on.

So my first ever appearance on the Melbourne stage had involved the setting on fire of a bucket, the destruction of an expensive lighter which had perished in the blaze and the transforming of an atmospheric theatrical moment into coarse comedy. Not a good start.

After much thought, they let me back on stage the next night and I managed to finish the season without destroying anything else.

The next job was to find an agent. And again, circumstances conspired in my favour. Magpie's production of *Funerals and Circuses* was finally coming to Melbourne. It was a good showreel for me as I played two completely different roles. This, surely, was my entree into the Melbourne acting world. If I could only get some agents to come along ...

This proved very difficult. Most agents were inundated with requests for representation and were not very keen on considering yet another. Eventually one agent reluctantly conceded she was coming to the show anyway, and while she definitely wasn't coming to see me, she supposed it would be difficult not to watch my performance. But she couldn't promise not to try. Or words to that effect.

And again, after the show, a phone number and an agent. So, no recipe for getting an agent I'm afraid. Again, it was just dumb luck. They do say that **the harder you work, the luckier you get,** but I don't know that that's true in my case. I was just in the right place at the right time.

I suppose you could say that I had not given up. I refused to go away. I gave myself every chance. And the more places you are in, the greater the chance of being in the right one at the right time.

Blue Heelers

Funerals and Circuses came and went. But more importantly I was finally in Melbourne. With representation. I started the process of inveigling myself into the fabric of the city, and at last I managed to get an audition for an episode of *Blue Heelers*.

Blue Heelers was an Australian police drama. Set in the fictitious country town of Mount Thomas, it was the equivalent of *Midsomer Murders* from the United Kingdom, a small undisturbed hamlet where there was at least one murder a week.

I still remember the audition scene, or at least one line from the scene. My character is being interrogated.

'How did he seem to you?'

'He was twitchy, nervous.'

This to me is sloppy TV writing. It might look good on the page, but no-one speaks like this. In commas. You might say, 'Oh, he seemed a bit nervous.' Or even, 'He was twitchy. You know, a bit nervous.' But even then, once you've explained he was twitchy why would you repeat yourself? Unless the other character didn't understand what you were saying. And that's a different scene. It's unnecessary verbiage, it might look impressive on the page, but you never speak in commas in real life.

So the actor that has to say that line is going to seem a little artificial. And even if the audience don't know exactly why, the performance won't seem completely truthful.

Thirty years later, I received an audition for another Aussie drama and the scene contained exactly the same line. 'He was twitchy, nervous.' Perhaps it was the same writer. Perhaps they didn't realise. Perhaps they did, but they didn't care. Perhaps they were bringing out the big guns: 'This'll impress them! Two adjectives!'

I would hesitate to say that the standard of TV writing hasn't improved over the years – I think it has – but too often the audition process is about trying to make awkward dialogue sound credible.

I have no qualms about changing dialogue in auditions. Within reason. If it's a small change, they'll just think you got the line wrong, and they won't particularly mind. They're more interested in whether you're right for the part than if you can be word perfect. And if it sounds more natural, then you're one step ahead of the competition.

At any rate, I must have managed to make those adjectives sound truthful since I got the part.

The role was a roo shooter. I am not a roo shooter. In fact were you to construct a human being unlike a roo shooter in every possible way, you would end up with something not unlike myself. I am an indoors sort of person, not an outdoors one. I'm not that keen on killing animals and anything that takes me away from the comforts of civilisation is to be avoided. I went into a mild panic. 'What's a roo shooter like?' I asked myself. And this was the point I started to go down the wrong path. I decided a roo shooter was tough and laconic, the silent type. And with that, I landed myself in stereotype-world. These are very broad brush strokes and nothing interesting is going to come out of them.

The question I should have asked is 'What would I be like if I was a roo shooter?'

And this sends me down a much more interesting and truthful path. I start to imagine how I got there. (How *I* got there, in all my idiosyncratic glory.) Perhaps I was the son of two schoolteachers who found themselves in a little country town and when I finished school I needed to find a job and roo shooting was the only thing going. I'm personally quite introverted, so perhaps I quite like being by myself out in the bush. Perhaps I have grown to find the town quite intimidating. I need to be constantly using my mind, so I might have become interested in the stars, spending nights out in the bush by myself with nothing else to look at. Perhaps I've become a bit of an amateur astronomer. I might have bought a telescope that I take with me when I go out shooting.

We're getting a little specific here, but the point is that I'm now creating a backstory. My work is going to be coming from something personal. It's going to be a truthful performance because it's based on my own self and it's going to be a unique performance, because I'm the only me in the world, and it's going to be an interesting performance because it is truthful *and* unique.

And yes, some of the things I have found are similar to the stereotype of the roo shooter. I'm still the silent type for instance. But that doesn't matter – my personal roo shooter is silent in a much more rooted and real way than the caricature because I've found the reason behind the silence.

And 'interesting' doesn't necessarily mean bizarre – it's important not to shy away from decisions about character that seem uninteresting. **The search for interesting can often lead us into external and untrue performance.** It's more important that the choice seems right and true than that it seems interesting.

No matter how far away from us the character seems, it's never completely alien. We all have a roo shooter in us, and a king and a mother and a teacher and a sex worker and a clown and even a murderer. It's only the circumstances that prevent us from realising these possibilities. It's our job to imagine ourselves into the circumstances and play the result.

This is the real character work. Sometimes we feel we need to think about walks and accents and physical shapes, but it's that use of the word 'if' that is the crucial thing here. It takes us back to ourselves, puts *us* into the experimental environment of the given circumstances and what develops from there is the character.

Of course, I realised all of this too late. If you ever come across that particular episode, skip on to the next one. Nothing to see here.

The difference between 'What is a roo shooter like?' and 'What would I be like if I was a roo shooter?' seems trivial, but one sends you into cliché and the other leads you down a very rich and rewarding path.

At any rate, massively unprepared, I turned up for a read-through of the script and rehearsals. My first guest role on Australian TV.

Most of my scenes were with William McInnes, one of the regular cast. William had been on the show for some time. He was obviously slightly bored and in need of entertainment. Which, to be fair, he provided himself. In fact he spent the entirety of the rehearsals speaking in an Indian accent. It was difficult to get a handle on the scenes, given that my character was supposed to be talking to a dinki-di Aussie copper, and yet I was actually rehearsing with a gentleman from the subcontinent. I found this strangely comforting. It reminded me of my Footlights days when anything was justified in the name of humour. Even accents of dubious taste. I have worked with William several times since then. It is always an amusing exercise and I look forward to the next. I survived the rehearsal and waited for my first day of filming.

Work as a guest artist is the most common sort of gig for Australian TV actors. It's not quite as glamorous as it looks. The audition script comes in three or four days before the audition, which doesn't give much time to go to the casting agent, read the script (if it's available) and work on the scenes. If and when you get the job, you are expected to be available across the period of shooting, perhaps two weeks, although you won't be needed for the whole time, usually a couple of days, sometimes just one, and if you're really lucky, more.

TV drama in Australia is run on a shoestring budget compared to the United States, so scenes are scheduled according to location. And as guest actors are paid by the day, you pray for a character that appears in more than one place. Judges are not remunerative, for example, as generally they just sit in court, so even if you have several scenes, you'll probably only come away with one day's pay. I did a guest role on *Inspector Blake*, another ABC police drama, where I had five small scenes but each one in a different location and, as it turned out, each location was filmed on a different day. Five days of pay! Boom! As the poet says. But that's very rare.

On the first day of shooting I arrived at unit base. Several large bus/trailer things and trestle tables and chairs. People everywhere. Everyone seemed to know what they were doing except me, and there was no indication of whom I should present myself to. I asked someone walking past festooned with different coloured rolls of gaffer tape.

'You need to see Andy.'

Ah, very helpful. 'Who's Andy?' But he was off. Eventually I did find Andy and was bustled off to wardrobe and then make-up and generally absorbed into the complicated machinery that is a film or TV crew on set.

If you're coming into this environment for the first time, you're going to feel an outsider. The crew and regular cast work every day together. They start very early, they finish quite late. They eat together. They spend most of the day in close proximity to each other. They tend to become big families. Everyone knows everyone else, little rituals get developed, endless games of hacky sack get played in the breaks. If a phone goes off on set, the cry of 'Slab!' goes up. The culprit has to buy a slab of beer for after work drinks on Friday. It's a big, chaotic but hard working community.

Over the years, you get to know some of the cast and crew and it's not so confronting, but coming into it for the first time is always quite difficult. People are nice, but a little dismissive. It's not worth getting to know you properly because you won't be around for long. But here's your costume. Put it on and go into that trailer for make-up. Breakfast in ten minutes.

You will also be extremely stressed about giving a good performance. This is your only shot on this show. You want it to be good. You may not know anyone, but you will know your lines. Back to front and upside down. The regular cast won't necessarily. They will have settled into a rhythm, they'll know their characters inside and out but they may not even have learnt their lines until they come to do the scene. It's easy to feel like an outsider.

I survived the filming. My roo shooter was separated from his wife and children. I had come back into town, partly to see them, partly for some other nefarious purpose; the passage of time has blurred the niceties of the plot, and I had a couple of scenes where I was reunited with my children. In two different locations, happily. Later I went slightly mad with a gun and had to be talked down. At the time I was reasonably happy with it all. Despite not coping with the roo-shooting thing, I thought I had navigated the demands of the plot with some aplomb.

When the episode was aired, my mother rang me. 'It's quite obvious you don't have children, because you didn't have the faintest idea how to interact with them.' Yes, alright, thank you. But she was right.

The author with Luke Lennox and a gun. Unable to handle either. Blue Heelers. *(Photo courtesy of Media West 7)*

I was awkward and unconnected from them. I didn't seem that keen to see them and there was no sense that I was their father.

I had been too busy obsessing about what a roo shooter was to worry about anything else. Furthermore, I didn't have the shorthand of having experienced fatherhood myself and I hadn't done any imaginative work.

I should have imagined myself into the family situation and the circumstances of the break-up and the anguish of being separated from them. I should have thought through how much I loved them and how much I missed them, and how much I had looked forward to seeing them and how wonderful it was to be able to hug them now.

I should have committed to the situation. But I did none of this. And it showed.

The next time I worked with children, I had become a father myself. And all that imaginative work was done for me because I had lived it.

As there was a relaxed attitude to actors returning to *Blue Heelers* in different roles, it was a good source of occasional work as a guest.

I came back five times as different characters, first the roo shooter, then an accountant, an ambulance driver of a religious bent, the owner of a security firm and finally a hobby chicken farmer. Fortunately no-one penetrated my various disguises.

Strangely (or not) the character of the security firm owner gave me the most trouble. I really couldn't work him out. He was just words on a page and I had no idea how to play him. I eventually gave up and turned up for shooting on my first day with the sinking feeling that I was a fraud and today everyone would realise it.

'If you could just pop into Wardrobe, Francis. Cheers.'

And with a sense of foreboding I climbed the steps to the trailer to discover that the head of wardrobe had chosen a purple shirt and a colourful tie for me and when I put them on and looked in the mirror, it was as though a door had been opened and I suddenly realised what sort of person he was and how I should be playing him. Brash. And confident. And no-one unmasked me as a fraud.

But like most actors, I'm still waiting.

It's not the first time that costume or make-up has saved me and it won't be the last, but it's good to realise that ideas come from everywhere, you just need to be open to them. And even though your character is your own possession and you have to look after it, **there are a lot of people connected with the show who have a stake in your character and you'd be a fool not to use them as a resource.**

I've had eureka moments from accent coaches and from designer's costume sketches. I've even got help from the call sheet on occasion.

The call sheet is the fount of all information: it has the scenes that are to be shot in the order that they will be shot, it tells you who is in the scene, the names and numbers of various members of the crew, where the location is, what time each actor needs to get there and even when lunch is. It's a very important piece of paper. But it also describes the scene to be shot. Generally in one sentence:

Richard tries to persuade Clarissa to elope.
David practices his Tai Chi and falls into the lake.
Jessica's pig ruins choir practice.

And so on.

This description is just the First Assistant Director's view of what the scene is and doesn't really have any significance apart from that, but more than once I've been reading the call sheet and suddenly had a blinding flash of insight into what the scene is about, which has pointed me in a slightly different direction than the one I was heading in.

Projection

I was a theatre actor. I had very little experience of screen. I had spent most of my professional life trying to hit the back wall of the Playhouse in Adelaide. My first scene on *Blue Heelers* involved an argument. And when we came to run through it on set, I didn't hold back.

'Jesus!' The sound guy hurriedly turned my microphone down. 'You don't hold back do you?'

And while I was sorry, I didn't really quieten down, and I haven't since. Obviously when I'm filming, I'm not trying to project my voice for stage – but I always give it both barrels. In one sense, there's no need. Microphones are so sensitive they can pick up someone dropping a handkerchief in the next suburb. You can mumble or mutter or whisper and you'll still be audible. So there's really no need to push it. And people do talk quietly in real life, so why shouldn't actors do it on screen?

However, the thing about projecting your voice is that not only does it give audibility, it gives energy. And bear in mind, that we're not talking about shouting here, we're talking projecting. Getting your voice to carry. When you bring your volume down it's easy to bring your energy down too. Or to put it another way, it's hard to keep up the tension when your voice production is minimal. And scenes become lifeless. Quiet and relaxed and natural but no zing.

I was once in a stage production that was unmiked. One of the actors, however, asked to be miked as he wasn't confident of his ability to project. The result was that he was certainly audible, but he didn't have to try to be. He ended up delivering the lines with much less dynamism than the rest of the cast and it made his performance oddly muted. And as he was the lead, the whole production became quite lifeless.

As I say, I've never tried to reduce my volume, and if I am a little loud at times they can always turn me down. But the energy of the performance is always there. And even when it's appropriate and desirable to whisper, I try not to let this affect the energy of the scene.

There is a growing trend to mike stage productions now. I can understand this for musical theatre when the actors have to compete with a band, but I think it's a pity otherwise. The energy of the performance is dissipated and as everyone's voices inevitably emerge from the same speakers, it becomes difficult sometimes to work out who is talking. And part of the actor's toolkit, an audible voice, is gone. We become less technically able.

Robert Menzies, one of Australia's great stage actors, regrets it too. He says there's something important about an actor's breath. That it's that breath that carries the sound that then reaches every member of the audience. One actor, on stage, pushing out air. And everyone receiving those vibrations. It's a lovely thought, and all that shared physical immediacy is lost when the sound comes out of a speaker.

Full Frontal

It was 1995. By this time, Shaun had moved to Melbourne too and was working on *Full Frontal*, a sketch comedy show on Channel 7. He got me an audition and I joined the cast.

Shaun went on to create some of the most hilarious television in Australian TV history – *The Micallef Program, Micallef Tonight, Welcher and Welcher, Newstopia, The Ex-PM* and *Mad as Hell* – and he took me along with him for every single one of them. Thank you Shaun. My gratitude is deep albeit rarely expressed. But I've always been slightly sensitive about it. A guest actor on *The Micallef Program* once asked me how I got cast on the show.

'Oh, I've known Shaun for years.'

'Ah, that's the way to do it, hey. Have a famous friend. I wish I had a mate who would cast me in things.'

Opens mouth. No reply presents itself. Closes mouth.

And for a long while I was quite troubled by the impression that I only got work because I was Shaun's friend. That people were thinking I shouldn't be there. And there have been other times as well, when I knew that I wasn't the director's first choice. That the guy who got the part had not been able to do it, for whatever reason, and that I had been the next in line. And that I didn't really deserve it.

But that way madness lies. **It doesn't matter how you got the part. What matters is what you do with it.** And that sort of thinking is not going to help you do the part properly, is it? So cut it out. You got the part. If you do a good job, no-one's going to care who got it first. And most people won't even know. So stop worrying about what's done and get on with it.

Full Frontal was an extremely popular show. And it raised my profile quite considerably. From extreme obscurity, I became, for the moment, a household face, if not a household name.

The show's demographic seemed to be twelve to fifteen year old boys. And among them I was an object, if not of slavish adoration, then at least obsessive interest. This paid off years later, when some of them started to produce their own shows and wanted to cast me in them as some sort of recompense for having given some meaning to their adolescent lives.

But at the time it was a little overwhelming. I remember being pursued down Elizabeth Street by a group of these incipient small screen producers, all shouting, 'That's him!' 'No, it isn't!' 'Yes it is!', until I had to escape into a bookshop to get away from them. They still followed me in and climbed up the shelves of the alcove next to me. And indeed, for as long as I was on the show, I was pursued by young male comedy enthusiasts wherever I went.

The thing was that they had nothing to say. They would rush up all aquiver, ask if I was on *that show*, and when I said yes, they would stand a little nonplussed for a second or two, realise that they didn't know what to do now and then mutter something and run off. The dog had finally caught the car and had no idea what to do with it.

There were a few who did manage to speak, however, but when they did it was inevitably to ask *that* question: 'How do you learn your lines?'

As I've said, I find it slightly depressing. I think it misses the point somewhat. But on the other hand, it is a valid question. There are the lines. You've got to get them from the page into your head. How do you do it?

The simple answer is you just do it. **You put your head down and concentrate. There's not really any other way.** I do it accumulatively. I read the first line. I put my hand over the script and repeat it. Then, when I'm satisfied I know that line, I learn the second line. And I put my hand over the script again and I say the first line followed by the second line. And when I've learnt up to there I go on to the third. And so on.

And the virtue of this method is that I find myself working on the lines as I try to remember them. 'This line is qualifying the line before', 'How would I feel if someone said that to me?' 'That doesn't sound right.' So the line and the interpretation come at the same time.

And interestingly, if I do find myself constantly tripping over the one line or group of lines, if they just won't go in, it's inevitably because I don't know how to play them. It's a little warning signal telling me I haven't understood them, intellectually or emotionally. And once I do stop to figure them out and commit to them, they stick in my head. ***If the line won't go in, it's probably because you're not doing it properly.***

Some actors record themselves and listen over and over. Some write them out again. One actor I worked with was dyslexic and found line learning very difficult. He used to write the first letter of each word. So:

'Like as the waves make towards the pebbled shore'

became

'L A T W M T T P S.'

It took him ages, but he swore by the method.

I find it much easier to learn lines once the scene is blocked. There's something about the marriage of line and physical position that really makes them just go in. I know that I say 'Come on, a cup of hot black coffee' while I'm bending over the other character. Then I slap him on the leg and move off while I'm saying, 'I'll put the kettle on.' I don't even have to go through the mental process of learning the lines. Just the fact that I've run through them a couple of times on the floor along with the blocking has made them stick.

For this reason, when I'm doing theatre, I never learn lines until I've blocked the scene. And then I make sure I learn them that night. So the next time I come to do it, the lines are there and I can concentrate on working the scene. Even if the blocking gets completely changed. Often, with the best of intentions, we don't get round to really getting the lines down until the last week of rehearsals. But the real work can only be done when the lines are down, and when you're looking at the other people on stage, listening to them and responding. So you've left yourself only a few days to get it all together.

And similarly, I would never learn the lines *before* rehearsal. The danger is you fix your performance and it becomes difficult to change it. Although I do know actors who do like to be word perfect on day one.

So learn your lines early, but not too early. Immediately after the first go at it. And then you put yourself in the best position to have plenty of time to work on the scene without having put yourself in a straitjacket.

People always expect comedy shows to be hysterical to work on. That's it's not really work and all you do is just sit around and laugh all day long. And there is certainly more laughing on comedy shows than in more serious shows. But they are work and they can be challenging. *Full Frontal*, for example, was not always a place of undiluted joy. There was a large cast, sketches were distributed every week and there was inevitably some dissatisfaction about the roles we were allocated. I was driven eventually (after a week where my contribution to the whole proceedings was just two lines) to beard the Chief Writer in his den and ask for a little more to do. He just laughed.
'I've had every single one of you in here this week complaining about how little they're getting. I really can't help you.'
Eventually, I came to the conclusion that I had to move on. I was going home after a day of standing in the background wearing a silly wig. It wasn't enough. I feel differently now – you'd have to drag me out by my feet, prising my fingers off the door frame, if you wanted to get rid of me.
And really, I was right then and I'm right now. I was just starting out back then, and I needed something more. And I left and I did other things. But priorities change and today, knowing the unreliable nature of the industry, I'd happily stay where I was. And try to get the most out of what I was given.
So after two seasons, I left and descended back into obscurity, and looked around for something else to do.

Macbeth

I managed to get cast in a Melbourne Theatre Company schools touring production of the Scottish play. I was to play Duncan, the Porter and various other minor parts. And a witch.

Being in a production of *Macbeth* means a lot of sitting around, unless you're Mr Mac, but this was a low budget production with a small cast and we all had several parts which kept us all reasonably busy. I discovered the Porter is a gift of a part – it's generally seen as the only comic relief in the whole play and the audience is usually very grateful.

I have a sneaking suspicion, however, that there is another scene that's intended to be comic: the banquet scene. It's classic farce. One minute Macbeth is greeting important guests and the next he's shouting at a ghost only he can see. Lady Macbeth runs around frantically, trying to rescue the situation. She assures the invitees that everything's fine. She takes Macbeth into a corner and tells him to pull himself together. Macbeth apologises, says that he hasn't been well, let's have some wine and what a pity Banquo's not here and in the next breath he's jumping on the table and screaming 'Avaunt and quit my sight!' It's the stuff of sitcoms. A sort of supernatural sitcom. I can see Frasier Crane doing it. Or Basil Fawlty.

The part I most enjoyed playing, however, was not the Porter, but Old Siward. Old Siward appears right at the end of the play. He is part of the force arrayed against Macbeth in the final battle. His main significance lies in the fact that he loses his son and seems completely unconcerned about it. And I think it's worth printing the scene in full.

The battle is over. Malcolm and the English have won.

> MALCOLM: I would the friends we miss were safe arriv'd
> SIWARD: Some must go off and yet, by these I see,
>   So great a day as this is cheaply bought.

MALCOLM: Macduff is missing and your noble son.
ROSS: Your son, my lord, has paid a soldier's debt.
    He only liv'd but till he was a man,
    The which no sooner had his prowess confirm'd
    In the unshrinking station where he fought,
    But like a man, he died.
SIWARD: Then he is dead.
ROSS: Ay, and brought off the field. Your cause of sorrow
    Must not be measur'd by his worth, for then
    It has no end.
SIWARD: Had he his hurts before?
ROSS: Ay, on the front.
SIWARD: Why then, God's soldier be he!
    Had I as many sons as I have hairs,
    I would not wish them to a fairer death.
    And so his knell is knoll'd.
MALCOLM: He's worth more sorrow,
    And that I'll spend for him.
SIWARD: He's worth no more;
    They say he parted well, and paid his score,
    And so God be with him! Here comes newer comfort.
        Enter MACDUFF *with Macbeth's head.*

When Old Siward learns that his son is dead his only question is whether he died in battle or running away. And when he learns that his death was in fact an honourable one, he seems to dismiss it completely. To the extent that when Ross sympathises with his loss he cuts him off and moves on.

However, it seems to me, and it seemed to me at the time, that far from being a moment of indifference, it is in fact a scene about a man refusing to give vent to an immense grief. Because his personal code and sense of honour demands he do so. Even the knowledge that his son has died can't shake him from how he thinks he should behave. And to be able to act this way in the face of such deep sorrow must take an enormous and heroic amount of strength.

I call this mastering of emotion Heroic Tension. I've stolen the term from Stanislavsky, without really examining how he uses it.

I hope I'm using it in roughly the same way as him, but if I'm not – I don't really care. This is how I understand the concept and it's helped me enormously over the years.

Heroic Tension is a concept that originates from the fact that it is more moving to see someone trying not to cry than to see them crying. As soon as I see anyone crying on stage or film, I tend to turn off a little. The moment before, when they have the impulse to cry and are trying to resist, I find infinitely moving, but once the waterworks start, I'm out of there.

Similarly, a character trying not to get angry is much scarier than a character that is expressing anger. The potential is there but the actual effect of the anger is left to our imagination. There is a moment in the film *Betrayal* where Ben Kingsley is confronting Patricia Hodge, his wife, with her infidelity. He seems, on the surface, utterly calm and then, suddenly, he does something with his hand, a little inadvertent flick of his fingers, Patricia Hodge flinches, and we understand that he is absolutely furious but that he has enormous self-control and he is, barely, keeping it in. I've forgotten a lot about that film, but I've always remembered that moment and that scene. It's a beautiful demonstration of Heroic Tension.

And again, seeing someone trying not to laugh? Hilarious. Seeing someone laugh? Meh.

So there's a tension between the emotion coming up from below and the struggle to contain it. And it's heroic, I suppose. And moving. And immediately engrossing. What's going to happen? Will the emotion win out or will the hero manage to control himself? Much more interesting than a simple, and often indulgent, outpouring of emotion.

And the emotion can be as big or as small as you like. From 'I'm slightly irritated but I'm going to be polite' to 'There's a tidal wave of anger or grief or whatever trying to get out but I'm absolutely determined not to let it and I'm using every bit of strength I have to keep it in.' Or from 'That's slightly amusing but I don't want you to see that I think so' to 'That's possibly the funniest thing I've ever heard and I'm desperately trying not to collapse into a heap of hysterical giggling.'

The bigger the emotion, the greater the strength needed to keep it in. And the more affecting and effective the moment becomes.

So Old Siward is a man who has lost the human he probably loved most in the world and yet he refuses to show his grief. It takes him a huge amount of strength to meet and equal the sorrow bubbling up from below and the scene now becomes both about grief and the extraordinary strength Old Siward needs to prevent himself from falling weeping onto the floor and *therefore* how tightly he holds up his personal code of honour. Even faced with the death of his son. And the scene is heartbreaking. Not only a moving representation of a man dealing with his son's loss according to his principle, but also a little counterpoint to the ease with which Macbeth dispenses with concepts such as morality and honour and his immortal soul.

And, of course, you can certainly play the scene as one where a father doesn't care about the death of his son, but why would you choose to? Why wouldn't you instead play a scene where a father battles his very deep grief because his personal code tells him his son has justified his life by dying heroically? Surely it's a better option and a more interesting scene?

The great advantage of using Heroic Tension is that it's a very truthful and accurate representation of what actually goes on when we are under emotional stress. We don't actually ever try to cry. (Unless of course we're using it as an emotional tool, and that's a completely different situation.) Most of the time we actually do try to suppress the emotion. We don't want to be seen to break down. ***So if, instead of trying to cry, because we think that's what the scene demands, we try not to cry, because that's what the character would do, we're going to end up with a more truthful scene.***

And if the tears do come in the end, well and good, but if they don't, it doesn't matter.

There's a myth that the mark of a good actor is being able to cry on cue, and writers love writing tears into the script, especially for female characters. But for my money, the actual crying is the least important part of the moment. And I'd rather see a single tear run down a cheek than any amount of sobbing and screeching and general breaking down.

Macbeth is supposed to be an unlucky play. Accidents happen when you put it on. It certainly has an eerie and malignant feel about it, partly, I suppose, because of the witches. And the Macbeth universe doesn't feel quite right. Immediately after the death of Duncan, an old man describes how nature has gone crazy. The normal order has been reversed.

'A falcon towering in her pride of place

Was by a mousing owl hawk'd at and kill'd.'

Fortunately none of us got injured during the run, but one evening, after an afternoon show in Kiama, as I drove the cast in our minibus through the darkening country roads back to Melbourne, a white owl flew down onto the middle of the road in front of me and, before I could register its presence, I had run it over. I don't know whether it was a 'mousing owl' or not, but it was quite upsetting. What was worse, five minutes later, another white owl landed in the middle of the road and the same thing happened. I can still see them landing and looking at me and hear the crunching sounds of the bus going over them.

Five minutes after that, we ran out of petrol.

Cue spooky music.

Blabbermouth

1996. Another role. I got a part in a children's show. *Blabbermouth* was based on the book by Morris Gleitzman and adapted by Mary Morris. Frances O'Connor played the main character. She has gone on to have an international film career in such films as *A.I. Artificial Intelligence* and *Mansfield Park*.

Another long season and, as often happens, the cast got restless. One matinee, fellow cast member Carole Patullo challenged us to take a coat-hanger on stage and justify its presence, but without changing the dialogue. Challenge accepted. Early on in the play, Carole was playing a thug. She unwound a coat-hanger, took it on stage with her and it became a tool for breaking into cars. Carole: one. Everyone else: nil.

I hit on the ingenious solution of making Carole my patsy. We had a scene together which involved Carole bringing on a pile of blankets and sheets. I secreted a coat-hanger in a folded sheet. The genius of the plan was that Carole would bring it on herself, and when she flung the sheet out onto the bed, the coat-hanger would fall out. She would realise what had happened, I would win the game and most importantly she'd probably lose control. She'd corpse (corpsing being the rather dramatic term for laughing on stage when one shouldn't). It was an ingenious and fiendish stratagem and it could not possibly fail.

The scene began. I felt slightly hysterical. Carole came on with the pile of sheets and blankets, the coat-hanger hidden inside, pulsating with comic potential. The moment approached, I felt the hysteria rising. Carole flung out the sheet and the coat-hanger fell on the floor. Tada! She looked at it impassively and continued on with the scene. Foiled.

I, however, was a complete wreck, almost non-functional with laughter and had to continue the scene with a pillow held in front of my face, to conceal my unsuccessfully stifled giggles from the audience. It was a very embarrassing moment and I felt ashamed of myself afterwards.

So ashamed in fact that I have never, ever corpsed since and any time that I can feel it happening, I remind myself of how unprofessional and amateurish it is and that snaps me out of any incipient hilarity.

Corpsing comes from a failure to commit completely. It often occurs in intimate scenes, where we might be meeting some obstacles to truly committing to the moment. We see the other actor rather than the character they're playing and we're suddenly outside the moment, looking at the situation and finding it amusing or embarrassing, rather than being *in* the moment. And perhaps that's the way to deal with it. **Remind yourself that this laughter is a sign that you're not committing to the action or the situation sufficiently**. That your work is, at this moment, effectively shit. Apologies for the language, but it's hard to fight off laughter. You need to shock yourself out of it. And the thought that you're not doing a very good job at the moment, that you should be ashamed of yourself, is one way to do so.

Corpsing does have one thing going for it: audiences love it. In moderation. It's a reminder that the play is happening just for them, at this very moment and that it won't happen like this again and they're privileged to see it. It reminds them that live theatre is quite dangerous, like walking a tightrope and it doesn't take much to bring everything tumbling down. It's so attractive to audiences that stand-up comics will often use it as part of their schtick – they pretend to find what they've said amusing and even to laugh at it. Or more likely, try not to laugh. It's the principle of Heroic Tension again.

And some actors will even do it on stage. Deliberately. And the audience, if they don't realise that this happens at this point every night, will lap it up. And I must confess that Shaun and I have done it ourselves. In a university revue sketch that wasn't getting any laughs, so we had to resort to corpsing to get any response. And even though we were young and callow and didn't know any better, I'm not proud of it. And I wouldn't do it again. It's okay for stand-up but not for anything else.

Navigating

That same year, I was offered a part in a play for Sydney Theatre Company. *Navigating* by Katherine Thomson. It was a beautiful play about whistleblowers and starred Noni Hazlehurst as Bea in her return to the stage after doing TV for approximately a million years. And Graeme Blundell, ditto. I played Brent, in love with Bea's sister and driven to terrorise Bea in the play's climax. I don't know why I was offered it, but I'd never worked at the STC and I was delighted.

There was one catch. 'You have to be considered a Sydney actor.'

Working interstate is an expensive business. You have to keep up rent/mortgage payments in your home state and pay for accommodation where you're working. For this reason interstate actors get paid an extra payment in cash, their 'per diems', for food and accommodation. Hence my problem. Being considered a Sydney actor meant that there wouldn't be any per diems and I'd have to pay for two places to live and food and transport all on one small theatre salary.

'But I'm a Melbourne actor.'

'Well, they say they'll just get someone from Sydney if you ask for per diems.'

And that's the actor's dilemma. If you don't accept these unsatisfactory pay and conditions then there's literally dozens if not hundreds of actors who will. I wanted the job, so I agreed. I found a flat in Darlinghurst and kept paying rent in Melbourne. It was a difficult time. In the end I was surviving on only two meals a day. I would get up as late as possible, have breakfast, miss lunch and then eat a cheap dinner in the Sydney Opera House cafeteria before the show. One member of the production took pity on my out-of-town state and suggested going out for coffee. My only panicked thought was that I would have to pay for the coffee which would eat into my funds and I made an excuse not to go. I still feel bad about it.

This shouldn't happen. If you're asked to work interstate then you should be paid accordingly. But it does happen. Quite a lot. Not to established actors, because administrators know they wouldn't get away with it. It's generally those just starting out who get put into this position. And then it becomes a guessing game: how much do I want the job and how much do they need me and will they really cast someone else? And inevitably the desire for the job wins out.

The author, showing no ill-effects from his starvation diet, with Graeme Blundell in Sydney Theatre Company's Navigating, *1998. (Photo: copyright Tracey Schramm)*

I'm glad I did *Navigating*. And in retrospect, the money issue gets forgotten. But I wouldn't accept such a deal now, and I doubt it would be asked of me. And it's one of the things that still annoys me – no-one asks administrators to take a pay cut. But actors are expected to.

This is a powerless profession. You don't get to choose when you work or what you work on or even what character you're going to play. And you certainly don't get to choose how much you get paid. At least in the beginning.

Another good reason to join the union.

Introducing Gary Petty

By now I had met and married a lovely Melbourne girl called Louise. Our daughter, Charlotte, came along in 1999. The work didn't. At least not often. Auditions were rare and offers even rarer. I started to regret leaving *Full Frontal*. I was in the middle of one of those unavoidable periods of inactivity that all actors have to face. I rang my agent to discuss matters and she revealed that as far as the agency was concerned they saw me as principally suited for TV commercials.

This was gobsmacking. TV commericals pay reasonably well but the pay-off is that your face is everywhere for a reasonably long time. And you're inevitably doing something stupid or humiliating. It may be a good advertisement for the product, but it's never a good advertisement for you. Apart from the fact that they're very hard to get. Usually the client has the final say in casting and so being cast in an ad is like winning a slightly dubious lottery. At any rate, this was not where I wanted my career to go.

I should have left the agency then. They obviously were not interested in finding work for me. Or at the very least I should have told them that I was not happy with this. But I didn't dare. It was a fairly prestigious agency and they were a little intimidating.

We are too often scared of our agents. I know actors who don't dare ask their agents to do the tiniest thing for fear of annoying them. Unfortunately, and this is especially so when we are just starting out, we feel that we don't have the power to control our own lives. And sometimes we actually don't. As I've said, it's a powerless profession. But we need to remember that **we employ our agents. They don't employ us.** We give them a percentage of our wages in return for them liaising with employers, organising auditions and negotiating contracts. They work for us, not the other way around.

As it turned out, a few years later they let me go. I found another agent quite quickly and was in the long run much happier. But as in any unsuccessful relationship, it still rankles that I wasn't able to dump them before they dumped me.

I'd met Matt Cameron when he was a writer on *Full Frontal* and he came to the rescue. He was directing a TV show called *Introducing Gary Petty*. It was co-written by himself and comedian Bob Franklin and he cast me as Edwin, a gay taxi-driver who was secretly in love with Gary. Gary Petty, played by Franklin, has a list of everyone who ever wronged him in the past: the girl who was mean to him in primary school; the cubby house club that wouldn't let him join; the parrot that insulted him in a pet shop, et cetera. Each episode involved him finding one character from his past, trying to get even and ending up with egg on his face.

It was a great concept, bedevilled by lack of funds. The café we shot in refused to close down while we filmed, or rather the production didn't have the money to pay them to close down, forcing us to film a substantial part of the show in a noisy café and making it almost impossible to subsequently hear the dialogue. Adding insult to injury, lack of time for scenes meant that we had to sit around the table in the order that said our lines while the camera panned across us. A pity, since it was a lovely idea and a strong script and Bob was extremely effective as the petty Petty.

In the last episode, I had a monologue straight to camera, which included the line: 'Gary planned it like a military campaign. I don't know if he had any ambitions in that area. I do know he wore a lot of camouflage.'

I did not like this line. It was a terrible line. I should never have had to say the line. I really didn't like it. It was terrible. And I was right, the line did sound terrible, but the problem wasn't with the line itself, as I discovered when I communicated my feelings to Matt. He looked at me.

'I think you should just try to commit to it, Francis.'

The idea that it was my fault, not the writing's, was shocking. But after I had recovered from my indignation, I realised that Matt was right, I hadn't been committing to the line. I had been rushing over it ironically and a little apologetically. And that's why it wasn't working. The next take I did commit to it, and the line worked. And if you ever manage to see the episode, I think you'll agree that it's an amusing line.

It took me back to Steven Gration's mantra, that you can make anything work if you want to. A lesson I thought I had learned but one I had obviously forgotten. And not for the first time. Perhaps there's something about this industry, that ***we're constantly learning things that we already knew.*** We are continually having to go back to first principles, making the same mistakes that we made in the past, realising that we'd already learnt that particular lesson and having to learn it all over again.

Or perhaps it's just me.

At any rate – committing. One of the most important tools in an actor's toolbox. You can go a long way just on committing. Forget about technique, or emotional connectivity or insightful text analysis, ***if you completely commit to what the character is doing or going through you're more than halfway there.***

No amount of technique et cetera will compensate for the fact that you're not completely entering into the situation.

And I often find that whenever a moment isn't quite working, it's usually solved by committing more fully to the action.

Man the Balloon

By 2001, Simon Phillips was the Artistic Director of the Melbourne Theatre Company. He commissioned Matt Cameron to write a play, two worlds intersected and I was cast in it. The play was *Man the Balloon*, a slightly absurdist play about a small town where the inhabitants start exploding. I played the local priest, Father Pagan, and Hector, an aggressive waiter. Jane Turner, one half of the extraordinarily successful duo *Kath and Kim*, was in it too.

I love being an actor and being in a play is a wonderful experience, but it's not all cakes and ale. And you don't always come to the theatre suffused to the brim with the love of Thespis and burning to get on stage and commune with the audience. This is work and sometimes you don't feel like going to work. And sometimes it's hard work.

During a matinee one Saturday, waiting to go on, I felt stuck. I was just about to go on as Hector and discover Rosemary Schmelliot's legs. Then I had to go off, get changed quickly, come back on as Father Pagan and find the legs again. Exit as Father Pagan and ten minutes later come back on as Hector and smack Herb Schmelliot in the head. Go off, come back with the accordion, wait for the explosion special effect and disappear, get changed back into Father Pagan, conduct a funeral service, come off, get roped together with Jane Turner and go on again to explode again et cetera et cetera et cetera. Then there were three hours to go before the evening show. And I had to do it all over again. It was all too much. I felt exhausted already.

I suddenly realised that looking forward made time pass much more slowly. The fact that I was focused on the things that I still had to do made me feel like I was on a train track and it became unendurable. I decided to focus on the moment. What was I doing now? I was getting ready to go on as Hector. What did I need to think about? What had Hector just done? What did he want? What did he expect to happen when he entered?

I placed myself in the present and time disappeared. And not only that, I could change what I was doing – I could bring Hector on in slightly different ways, either emphasising his irritation or bringing it in check – and the play became a place where change and spontaneity were possible, rather than a sequence of fixed events that I had to get through.

Since then, I've never, ever allowed myself to think ahead. Unless I'm setting props. And if I find myself doing it, I force myself to stop and I start to think about the present moment. Or what I'm just about to do. And I can honestly say that I've never gone through that feeling of being stuck on a railway track again.

A short while later Matt Cameron asked me to take part in a little radio sketch segment. It was part of a program about writing comedy. A sketch about a father and son. I played the son and Ross Williams, another *Full Frontal* alumnus, who had also been in *Man the Balloon*, played the father. It was quite a dark piece and at the end of the recording I noticed the radio presenter was looking at me quite strangely.

'I'm interested in your choices. You played it quite straight. Why did you choose to do that?'

I didn't know how to answer the question. I had just played it in the way I saw it. I hadn't made any choice as far as I was aware. I mumbled something unsatisfactory and left.

'Choices' is a term that is often used in a theatrical sense. 'He makes good choices.' 'I'm not sure about some of your choices.' Et cetera. I've never liked the word. To me it implies that I've considered several options and plumped for this one. Stammer or lisp? Sexual tension, mild revulsion or barely contained insanity? I don't think it works like that. It may look like you've made a choice because you're doing the role in a way that the viewer didn't think of, but in reality all you've really made is a decision.

For me, there only seems to be one way to play things. I never consciously weigh-up two options. I read the scene or the play and something occurs to me, and it seems right and I go with that. Sometimes nothing occurs to me, and I need to do more work. Sometimes my approach leads me down a dead end and I have to rethink things. But I don't think I've ever come up with two ideas and then had to discard one.

I think it's to do with being good at interpreting texts. The more able you are to understand what the scene is trying to do, what the character is trying to do and what the playwright is trying to do, the better your ideas will be and the more they will suit what's down there in black and white.

'He has good ideas.' That would be a lovely thing to hear. Or 'His work is truthful and interesting and yet it really suits the play.'

But 'He makes good choices?' What, he went for butter instead of canola oil spread? *No, I don't make choices. I do what I think the text is asking for.*

A small point, but it bugs me.

In this case, even though the form was a sketch, the scene was quite dark. And written in a naturalistic style. It seemed to be asking me to play it truthfully. I don't know what the radio presenter was expecting but to play it in a comic way would be to completely undermine the writing.

It's the first principle of comedy. *Don't play funny. Play for truth.* There's nothing worse than watching someone act with the consciousness of being funny. Look at Buster Keaton. You couldn't get a more serious dude. And he's hilarious.

Or to put it another way. *There's no difference between 'comic acting' and 'dramatic acting'.* Everything that's important in Strindberg or Mamet or Caryl Churchill – intention, commitment, emotional connection – is just as important in Wilde and Neil Simon and David Williamson. You need to commit to the moment. You need believable and truthful characters. And if you don't approach comedy in the same way as you approach non-comic texts, then you won't engage the audience. And you may get laughs, but they'll be the wrong sort of laughs and the script as a whole won't sing because the audience aren't inside it. They're outside, waiting for the next funny thing.

Comedy is a broad church and it ranges from people in dinner suits being witty to loud farting sounds, but if there is one rule to bind them all, it's take it seriously. Don't act funny. And it's such a crucial point I'm going to repeat it. ***There's no difference between comic acting and dramatic acting. Don't act funny. Don't try to be funny. Honour the text.*** So there.

Babes in the Wood

In 2003 I had coffee with a man named Michael Kantor. He was about to direct a twisted pantomime for Playbox Theatre Company called *Babes in the Wood*. He was assembling his cast. Two years later Playbox would rebrand itself as Malthouse and Michael would be its first Artistic Director. I would become a part of his stable of actors. But that was all in the future, for now it was just a question of drinking latte and trying to impress him.

I don't know by what mysterious alchemy directors can make decisions about casting over a coffee. Rosalba Clemente had cast me in *The Club* on the basis of a brief chat and now Michael apparently saw enough in my incoherent and badly hidden desire to be employed to cast me as an emu named Flapgherkin, the idiot sidekick to the evil kangaroo Boingle. Boingle was played by one of Australia's national theatrical treasures, Julie Forsyth. Max Gillies, another treasure, dragged up to play the evil Aunty Avaricia and the cast also included Eddie Perfect who would go on to international fame as the composer of such Broadway musicals as *King Kong* and *Beetlejuice*.

Being a conscientious soul I took myself and my family off to the zoo to look at emus, to examine their physicality and peer into their souls. To find, as it were, the essence of the emu. It was a disappointing trip. The temperature was in the high 30s, the children were fractious and the emus were not disposed to be helpful. In fact they just stood there. Occasionally they would turn their heads and look at something, and once or twice they took a step or two. This was not much to work with.

The show began with just the two of us, kangaroo and emu, moving around on stage. This was the first scene we looked at.

'Let's just run it', Michael said. 'See what happens.'

We ran it. Julie, of course, was already a hilarious and believable kangaroo. Lying down, scratching, moving, the whole bit. All I had was a head move and a step. But they do say do what you know, so I did that.

Michael came up to us. 'Great Julie ... Francis, what were you doing?'

'Well, this is what emus do on a hot day', I said, somewhat feebly. And fortunately the script did specify the day was quite a hot one.

'Oh, okay.' Slight bemusement. And we left it at that.

And in the end the scene worked brilliantly. The audience recognised the emuness of the moment and they loved it. It brought a couple of things home to me.

First, ***the power of stillness.*** How compelling standing still on stage is. And how it raises your status. How tiny movements become so striking if they come from complete stillness. And how distracting irrelevant motion can be, even if the audience isn't consciously aware of it. Like a certain actor's feet in *The Club*.

And secondly, and not unconnected to the first point, the old idea that 'less is more'. That you don't need to try too much if it's not needed – just do what's required.

There's a lovely little YouTube clip of actor William H. Macy talking about this. He says that he often hears actors say to him 'It's only a small part, but I think I can do something with it.'

And his response is, 'Oh, no. Don't do that. Don't "do something" with it. Just do the part.'

Often when we try to 'do something' with it, we end up not doing 'it'.

But if all emus do is stand still, then there's no point trying to add on to that. Just do what's required.

I felt out of my depth during rehearsals. Everyone seemed so confident and able and I didn't feel either of those things. We always started the morning with yoga and, while the other actors' bodies seemed to effortlessly flow into the required positions, I struggled to get my unlithe and lissomless mass of sullied flesh to twist even a quarter of the desired way round. And as for downward facing dog, it could go f... itself.

About halfway through rehearsals I had a chat with Iain Grandage, the musical director. 'It's a good environment', he said, 'because you senior actors aren't playing games.'

This hit me with some force. I remember being absolutely floored that I could be considered one of the *senior* actors. I looked around. There were Julie Forsyth and Max Gillies talking in a corner. Max was and is inextricably linked not only to the beginnings of theatre in Australia via his work with the Pram Factory but also the beginnings of Australian TV satire via his show *The Gillies Report*. If anyone's an icon in this industry it's him. Julie is one of the most respected actors in Australia. And with good reason. Both she and Max are brilliant performers and wonderful actors. And Iain was putting me in that group?

The subtle facial stylings of senior actors Max Gillies, Julie Forsyth and the author in Babes in the Wood. *MTC. (Photo: Jeff Busby)*

I looked around the rehearsal room, and it was true – the rest of the cast was, despite their confidence and talent, much younger than me. I realised I had accumulated a much longer CV than any of them. And while I was nowhere near the lofty levels on which Max and Julie resided, I was, relatively, senior.

That moment was the beginning of a real sea change for me. It didn't happen overnight, but I stopped thinking of myself as an interloper and started believing that I belonged. And slowly, I stopped getting so stressed. And relaxed. And, I believe, my work got better, because I was less worried about my place in the world and the industry and more concerned about what I was doing.

Not everyone has an Iain Grandage to give them perspective, unfortunately, but it's good to remember that **stressing about whether you belong and feeling inadequate are the enemies of good work.**

Sam

By this time Louise and I discovered ourselves the parents of twins, Sam and Isabel, and things became hectic. To add to the chaos of having three children under three years old, it became quickly apparent that Sam was not well. He refused to put on any weight and would often vomit his milk up. Next to Isabel, who was growing at an extraordinary rate, he seemed tiny. Eventually, after a series of paediatricians had seen and misdiagnosed him, he was sent for an MRI.

I was working on a TV show called *Marshall Law* at the time. Ostensibly a raunchy legal drama, it starred Lisa McCune, Alison Whyte and William McInnes. I played Gavin Duffy, the best friend of William's character. It showed promise, but never got into its stride and was not renewed for another season. It was probably, for me, anyway, a stroke of good financial luck that it didn't. As a regular guest actor on a TV drama, you are not given enough work to make ends meet, but you're expected to be on hand whenever the production decides they want you, which makes getting any other work extremely problematic.

I was on set, waiting for my scene when Louise rang from the hospital.

'Sam's got a brain tumour.'

I spent the next few hours, and probably the next six months, in a state of shock. I'd never had any experience of cancer. William came to the rescue, and got the day's schedule reorganised so I could go to the hospital. I'll always be grateful. I was in no state to organise anything.

The story of the operation and the subsequent rounds of chemo doesn't belong here, but five months after the diagnosis and at the age of nine and a half months, at 5 in the morning, Louise and I watched as Sam quietly died.

And again, the aftermath of Sam's going and how we all were and are affected, even including Edward who was born a year later, is the subject of another book, but to be absolutely, dispassionately, coldly analytical about it, one of its consequences was that I became a better actor.

For me Sam's death was, of course, the most devastating so far of all the blows that life inevitably deals out to all of us. Without wanting to seem unduly pessimistic, it's impossible to live a life without at least some setbacks and disappointments. Ill health, death of a loved one, the breakdown of a relationship, career hopes dashed – everyone goes through something, and I find that whenever I talk about Sam to anyone over 40 I immediately discover that they have their own story, just as tragic, if not more so, than mine.

So how does something like that affect my work? And how do I use the experience?

I've never consciously used Sam's death as a direct parallel to any character I've played. I did refuse to play a bereaved husband in a corporate improv, just after he died. It was too soon to confront those emotions publicly. I played a bereaved parent much later, on the TV drama *City Homicide*. I can't remember deliberately bringing Sam to mind at any point during the shooting. I thought about him, of course, but I didn't 'use' him on camera. I didn't have to, I knew the general situation intimately and all I needed to do was concentrate on the circumstances and the emotions just came. **Sam's death put me in the ball park.** I knew what the character felt, and I just had to play the moment.

What did change, and has changed for me after his death, was that there now seems to be a vast ocean of sadness, just below the surface, that I can access extremely easily. Perhaps it was always there, and those barriers to expressing emotions that we normally put up have been worn down by extreme grief. Perhaps I'm just a sadder person, having lived through the death of my child. But whatever the reason, I became a more emotional actor. Or an actor with a readier access to my emotions. I think the process of living and coping with the slings and arrows does this to us anyway, and perhaps it was slightly accelerated in my case. Perhaps there's no escaping the wearing down of our natural defences against expressing emotion and the passage of time inevitably makes us better actors.

I think also that if there has been a journey or an arc, in my development as an actor, it's the journey from being an actor that works from the outside in, to one that is happy to work from the inside out. Sam's death, I think, really flipped me into the latter camp.

After the last final diagnosis, we took Sam home, and at the end of two weeks, as predicted by the doctor, he went into a coma. We were told this would last a couple of days, and again, the timing was spot on. In the evening of the second day, Sam's breathing changed dramatically. Something was obviously about to happen and I remember saying to Louise:

'I think he's going to die tonight.'

And at that moment I realised that not only wouldn't he be around tomorrow, but that I was entirely unprepared for it. His absence. And it really was the proverbial bolt of lightning. We had known for a fortnight that Sam would definitely die and the possibility had been real and increasing all the way through the five months of his treatment, but until it was actually about to happen, I had not the faintest inkling of what it would be like when he was actually gone.

So, perhaps the death of someone near to you is one of the few experiences you can't imagine your way into if you haven't personally experienced it. Or perhaps I just have a feeble imagination. But for me at least, there was no substitute for experience. Unfortunately.

It seems so long ago now and the other three children are nearly adults, but I only have to talk or think about Sam for a few minutes and I start to cry again. It's something that never goes away. And though I can't really, even now, accept this viscerally; intellectually, at least, I know that I'm lucky. I'm lucky as a human to have had that experience. To have known Sam and to have been with him when he died. And lucky as an actor too.

Take Away

Later the same year, I was offered a role in a film. It was called *Take Away* and starred Vince Colosimo and Stephen Curry. This was a bit of good news after the drama of the past months and I allowed myself to get quite excited. However, when I received the script and started to eagerly turn the pages in search of my character's name, I saw, to my chagrin, that I was in the first two minutes of the film and then I completely disappeared.

No matter, I was in a film. I was playing an innkeeper in a flashback explaining the derivation of the dim sim. And I was going to be the funniest innkeeper ever seen in a flashback explaining the derivation of the dim sim. I practised and practised. I gave him a funny voice. I did lines in a funny way. I moved funnily. It was all going to be the height of hilarity. I was ready.

When we ran through it prior to shooting, I gave it both barrels. To my surprise, the director, Marc Gracie, wasn't impressed.

'Can we cut the voice Francis? Just your normal voice is good.'

I was quite affronted. I'd worked hard on the voice. I knew funny and the voice was funny. However, I still had my funny walk. All was not lost. We did a first take.

'Can you do that walk more normally, Francis? If you just do it straight, that's all we need.'

And on it went. By the end of the day, my performance had been gutted and I was left, as I saw it, with no character at all. I went home in a huff. Which was strange since I'd arrived in my car. But whatever the mode of transport I was furious. How could Marc do that to me? I wasn't being allowed to do my thing. Didn't he cast me to be funny in the first place?

But when I'd recovered from my professional petulance enough to watch the scene, I realised that Marc had been right. Instead of there being no character left, there was a truthful and amusing portrayal of an innkeeper who had been put on the spot. Marc had forced me to play the moment. To play the truth of the situation instead of trying to be funny. It was the perfect demonstration of the benefits of not trying to be funny but honouring the text and letting the scene be funny. Another lesson forgotten and relearned.

This is the difference between the comic actor and the comic performer. One serves the text and one gets laughs.

The action in the script is to walk down the street, not notice a banana skin on the ground, step on it, and slip over. The comic actor will carry out the action as truthfully as he or she can. You will see someone walking down the street in a believable and non-comic way, they will truthfully carry out the action of not seeing the banana skin, they will step on it. You'll see someone surprised and then dismayed as they fall over. And if it's a comedy, you'll laugh because of the situation or the context: perhaps they threw the banana skin out of the window themselves, perhaps they've just taken someone down a peg in an unpleasant way and here's their comeuppance, perhaps they've only just conquered a phobia of bananas. But you're laughing because the script works. The actor has made it work.

The comic performer will walk down the street in an amusing way. When they step on the banana skin, their reaction will be hilarious and their falling over ridiculous and we will laugh because they are funny *over and above the script.*

Both got a laugh, so what's the problem?

Well, the problem with the comic performer's *modus operandi* is that we have been taken out of the story. We are now standing outside laughing at the way it happened, not the action itself. The fact that the character was scared of bananas is irrelevant. All that work to set up their phobia? Pointless. All we're thinking about is how funny the actor is. And moreover, now that the audience has come out of the story, it may not be possible to get them back. So we've weakened the story and we've got ourselves a disengaged audience.

The fact that the audience laughs is not a justification for what you've just done. Not all laughs are good laughs.

Of course, if the script is weak to start with, honouring the text as the comic actor does is not going to elicit laughter and so then perhaps the comic performer is justified in creating a laugh, but if we're going to second guess the script before we even put it in front of an audience, we're defeated before we start.

And of course, if the comic performer is not getting their laugh then we're in even bigger trouble.

If you want an example, I'd say that Steve Carell is a comic actor while Will Ferrell is a comic performer.

And obviously this is a huge generalisation. In reality, the line between the two is blurred. Or rather they are the two ends of a spectrum that all actors move along. But I've always felt that the comic actor is the more noble profession and, while it's great to get laughs, audiences want more than that. They want the story, they want to feel, they want meaning. And that's what the comic actor gives them.

The Odyssey

2005 and another Michael Kantor show. It was playwright Tom Wright's version of *The Odyssey*. I found myself reunited with Paul Blackwell. Stephen Phillips played Odysseus. And a young actor called Ben Lewis joined the cast. He would go on to have an international career, playing the lead in *Phantom of the Opera* on the West End.

I played Antiphus, one of Odysseus' crewmen. My character was not a major one and therefore not particularly fleshed out, as the writer himself acknowledged. I looked at the lines. Most of them were quite functional, 'Look out!', 'What's that sound?' et cetera, but there did seem to be a common thread. They seemed to all be about safety, keeping your head down and staying out of trouble.

I went to Michael and asked if I could give all my lines to other characters, perhaps just keeping one line, 'Have faith!', which might be quite effective if it was the only time he spoke and would serve as his personal mantra. Trust Odysseus, keep your head down and we'll get home.

Michael is very much in the camp of those who see the writer as simply another contributor and so lines can be cut or reworked in rehearsal at the drop of a hat. This could make life difficult if you were basing your character on lines that were subsequently cut, but in this case it worked for me and he agreed.

I grew a long bushy beard and created a silent, watchful, awkward figure. He came across as slightly sinister and I was quite pleased with the result. It's not always the lines that matter.

Michael was enormous fun in the rehearsal room. I worked with him on several shows. They were always spectacular and crowd pleasing and I enjoyed just about every single one I was in.

Except this one.

I found the rehearsal process very difficult. As the days went on, the whole production seemed set against me. I was convinced Michael was hating what I was doing and I got more and more disheartened and paranoid. Looking back on it now, it's quite clear that Antiphus was having an effect on me. Playing a suspicious, silent loner was turning me into a suspicious, silent loner. I wish I had realised it at the time as I would have been able to intellectualise myself out of my mood, but I couldn't see the wood for the trees and I just gritted my teeth and went on.

This bleeding of one's character into one's everyday life is very common. No matter how careful or how experienced you are, it's very difficult to avoid taking home at least a vestige of the person you've been trying to become during the day. Years before, during rehearsals for *The Club*, I had developed a high-pitched squawk for Ted when he became more than usually stressed. The line 'Tradition, tradition, tradition!', in particular, often reached a pitch that only nearby dogs could hear. I remember having an argument with my girlfriend at the time about precisely this issue of bringing the character home. She accused me of being Ted after work. I was outraged. This was a complete lie.

'You do, you act like Ted.'

'No, I don't!!!' I squawked.

And in the distance an aggrieved beagle could be heard woofing its distress.

But it's not just emotional baggage that gets carried around. Sometimes the baggage has a physical form. Well, duh. What I mean is that you can take home the physical stuff as well as the emotional. My mental patient in *Marat/Sade* played the clarinet. And the recorder. I gave him a constant finger wiggle. Unless he was playing, his fingers were constantly on the go, as though he was playing the piano, or typing. The idea was that he was only truly at peace when he was playing his instruments. But once I had it in my bones it became second nature. I would do it even when I wasn't on stage and the rest of the cast were constantly saying 'Francis, fingers!' to remind me to stop. And it took me a couple of weeks after the season ended to finally get rid of the tic.

Nowadays I'm much more careful about bringing home characters and, within the parameters of having to take work for financial reasons, I try to avoid characters like Antiphus that are going to cause me grief. Much later, when I got to do *The Odd Couple*, I was determined not to be Felix, the hypochondriac obsessive compulsive neatness freak. I really did not want to take him home. In the end I discovered that the grumpy depressed slob, Oscar, was no picnic either and that perhaps I should have chosen differently. At least the house would have been cleaner.

The author, in paranoid mode, wondering why everyone is looking at him. With Paul Blackwell and Ben Lewis in The Odyssey. Malthouse. *(Photo: Jeff Busby)*

But I'm giving the impression that this process is bad. It's not really. It shows the character is living inside you. And it's caused by our old friend empathy. The most important quality we can have as an actor. And as I've said, one of the hardest to really assimilate.

But all the same, it's best to be aware that the character may come home with you. And to try to avoid it.

Things We Do for Love

In 2005, in another bit of good fortune, I was offered a part in an MTC play directed by playwright Aidan Fennessy.

'They're sending you the script to read and see if you want to do it.'

I was always quite amused whenever my agent said this to me. I appreciated the presumption behind it, that I was very busy and would only take a job if I liked the role. In reality, this was a complete fiction – I wasn't so overwhelmed with offers that I could afford to pick and choose. If a job came up, I took it. The alternative was not eating. However, I played along and said I'd read the script. It was a play by Alan Ayckbourn, *Things We Do for Love*, about the romantic entanglements of four people living in the one house. All three levels of the house were visible, the top of the basement, the entirety of the ground floor and the bottom two feet of the first floor. I played Gilbert, the caretaker, living in the basement and harbouring an untold passion for Barbara on the first floor, played by Pamela Rabe. Marco Chiappi and Roz Hammond, an old friend from *The Micallef Program*, rounded out the cast.

I think we were all a little contemptuous of the play when we started rehearsals – someone in the production confessed they'd thrown the play across the room after reading it – but the more we rehearsed it, the more we came to admire it. Ayckbourn is an absolute master of the theatre and being inside the play made us aware of how brilliantly he knows his craft and his audience.

I remember being concerned that there weren't enough gags in the piece and was constantly inventing extra ones. I needn't have worried. When we came to the first preview, it was obvious that the laughs were all there and they were where Ayckbourn intended them to be.

At one point in rehearsals, we were sitting round the table taking notes. Aidan was talking.

'Francis, I love it when you break up that li–'
Pamela broke in.
'Stop! Don't tell him! It'll ruin the moment!'
Astonished pause.
She went on:
'General praise. Specific criticism.'
It's hard sometimes to realise where and when you learnt something. And even what it is you learnt. But this was, when I had absorbed it, a bolt from the blue.

And Pamela was right. Once somebody, a director, for example, praises a specific moment, then they have changed forever the mental circumstances that have formed to create that moment.

The next time you come to do it, it is impossible not to think, 'Ah, this is the bit that Aidan likes', and immediately you're not doing what you were doing to create the moment in the first place. Which involves the given circumstances, what's just been said to you, your emotional connection to the moment, all sorts of things, but *not* any thought of anything outside the moment. Presumably.

And the moment is nearly always ruined.

I remember someone saying, 'No-one does gormless as well as you, Francis', after a particular take filming a scene for a TV show. I knew what they meant. They were referring to a particular moment where I looked nonplussed at what had been said to me. Not complicated.

But after that remark, I could never get it back again. Every time I came to do it, I couldn't help thinking about the praise I had got, and the moment had been destroyed.

General praise is fine.
'That scene's working well, now.'
'I think you're heading down the right path with the character.'
Or just 'Yes, good work guys.'

And criticism can be specific. In fact it should be. You're focusing on something that needs improving. You're asking the actor to concentrate on something functional, to stay inside the moment, not come out of it. Specific praise says that that moment doesn't need changing, and yet makes it impossible for it to stay the same.

I now always ask directors at the beginning of rehearsals not to give me specific praise. Slightly presumptuous, but what is an actor if not that?

At one point in the play the comedy comes to a screeching halt and Gilbert, slightly the worse for the drink, tells Pamela how he has come to love her since his wife died. It's a lovely speech and a moving one. During rehearsals Aidan told me that I should go deeper. And I knew what he meant. There was more to be made out of the speech. The stakes should be higher. It means a lot to Gilbert and to actually express it is a big thing too. All very clear.

But 'going deeper' sent me off in the wrong direction. I was back on stage as the bishop in *Marat/Sade* trying to excavate an emotion out of myself. Human beings don't behave like this. Digging deeper to find emotion is an activity that no-one did ever. Most of the time, as I've pointed out already, we try to repress emotion.

'She's a bit rude, but I won't say anything.'

'I've been waiting for my coffee for 20 minutes, but I'll be polite.'

'He looks hysterical bending over like that, but I can't laugh.'

And in fact, when we are in the grip of emotion, it comes in spite of ourselves. We try not to cry but we can't stop ourselves. Heroic Tension again.

This was the point when it all came together for me. When I realised that 'digging deeper' to try to dredge up some undislodgeable emotion didn't work. And that it might be better to concentrate on stopping it coming up. Prevent it, prevent it, prevent it ... and then let it out. The first way takes you down completely the wrong path. As I'd discovered when I did *Marat/Sade*. I should have played the scene as a man trying to restrain what was bubbling up inside him. Oh for a time machine.

And paradoxically, trying to repress emotion often makes it stronger. The harder you push it down, the bigger it gets. But at any rate, 'letting the emotion out' is probably a better way of looking at things. Or 'make it more difficult to say', or 'the stakes are higher' – but not 'go deeper'.

It's important to understand though that using Heroic Tension doesn't create the emotion to start with – that's about the given circumstances. Get those right and really connect with the situation and the emotion will come. And then Heroic Tension is a truthful way of controlling it.

So what I needed to do was to go back to the source. Do some more work on my backstory, make it more immediate – what was it like to lose my wife, what was my life like in the aftermath, how did I meet Barbara, when did I realise I was in love with her?

If the circumstances are right, the emotion will just come. And if I'm really understanding the circumstances, if I'm really empathising, the stakes will be high. And then perhaps, if instead of trying to dig emotion up, I try to restrain it, I'll be getting close to something real and true.

My character was from the north of England and we had an accent coach to help us get the accents right. Accents can be tricky. They are such precise things: the 't' needs to be a 'd' or this vowel needs to be produced at the front of the mouth, but this one at the back. There are so many little details to concentrate on. However, eventually it needs to come naturally. You need to be able to put the cloak on and walk around in it.

Interestingly, halfway through the rehearsals, the accent coach pointed out that the only moment where the accent really worked was in my drunk scene. My mind was on something else completely and the accent just came out.

I have done a lot of book narration over the years, and consequently had to do a lot of accents. Mostly I've come out the other end alive. Except for when a Scottish character was talking to an Irish character, when my brain exploded and I had to be helped weeping from the recording booth and given brandy. But the one thing I've found is that I get better at the accent as the book goes on. It becomes more and more organically part of me. And that's mainly to do with going for it. Over and above all the little details of voice production, the one thing that enables me to do an accent is committing to it.

As with most things.

Rehearsals for *Things We Do for Love* were hard and quite depressing. I could never quite get there. In fact, I've often found rehearsals to be difficult.

There's a story about Sir Laurence Olivier. During an interview, he was asked whether he enjoyed his career and his answer, strangely, was no. He said he found rehearsals challenging and depressing; and performing had been a constant battle; and apart from a couple of nights doing light comedy where everything went right, it had been very hard.

Now I don't want to compare myself with Sir Larry, but I feel the same way. Rehearsals for me have always been about struggling to bring something out of me, to create something new, which is always painful and not always successful. I generally go home after a day of rehearsals with a sense of having utterly failed to achieve anything. And the next day, I get up and it's a new day and I go into rehearsals determined to get something right this time. And I fail and I go home depressed. What does Beckett say?

'Try again. Fail again. Fail better.'

And then the first preview happens and you realise that you do have something, and it seems to work. But it's never perfect.

So if you are finding rehearsals difficult and you feel like you're not getting it, then well done. That's what you're supposed to feel. Relax. Well, don't relax too much, you open in two weeks. But just know that this is supposed to be difficult and keep on going.

Adding to my feelings of inadequacy during this rehearsal was the fact that the rest of the cast seemed to be at the top of their game. And none more so than Pamela Rabe in the central role of Barbara. There was one point during my drunk scene where I had to chase Pamela around the sofa. To my surprise, when we started rehearsing this scene, she wouldn't move. I would take a few steps towards her and she would just stay there. She didn't say anything, but she just would not go round the sofa. Eventually I went to Aidan.

'Aidan, she's not going round the sofa.'

He looked at me.

'I think you need to make her, Francis.'

And I realised that I wasn't really chasing her. I wasn't committing to the action (and here's another example of learning the same lesson over and over again). I didn't really want to catch her, I was just performing the empty gesture of moving towards her. A bit.

Pamela was too professional to direct me but she sure as hell wasn't going to do anything on stage that wasn't properly motivated. So she did nothing. And I got the picture. And the next time we rehearsed the scene I tried to catch her. And she moved.

You are the only one looking after your character. You have to make sure they are moving truthfully through the play. Don't let them do unmotivated acts just because it's convenient for the production. It's not being difficult, it's being truthful.

I lost my voice during the run. I don't think I was misusing it, I just got some sort of virus and all I could do was whisper. I felt terrible. Not so much physically as mentally. I hated the idea that the show would be cancelled and the company lose money because of me. A solution was reached. I would still go on stage and move around as Gilbert but another actor was hired to sit in the wings with the script and read the lines. And it really worked. Audiences love it when something goes wrong. It's like an actor corpsing. It makes the event they're attending completely unique and it's the area where live performance has it in spades over screen.

'I was there when the gun didn't go off.'
'I was there when the cup rolled into the audience.'
'I was there when your trousers fell down.'

In this case, they were witnessing something unexpected that we were trying to fix and they embraced the concept completely.

It's not something I'd like to do again. Looking beseechingly into Pamela Rabe's eyes while an offstage actor tells her he loves her in a Yorkshire accent is an interesting experience but once is enough. And the rest of the cast didn't enjoy it much either. I was on strict orders to rest my voice and, if I did try to talk, there would be an in-unison scream of 'Francis, be quiet!' And when my voice did come back it was a refreshing experience for people to be happy that I could talk.

One last memory of *Things We Do for Love*. I was on stage, my voice having miraculously returned, telling Barbara how much she meant to me, and it just wasn't working. No emotional connection, no being in the moment, no 'feeling it'. Just wallowing around in fakery and meaningless dialogue. Shithouse. Which is another of the poet's favourite sayings. I came off feeling wretched and Pamela turned to me.

'You know, Francis, that's the best you've ever done that bit.'

Just because you're not feeling it, doesn't mean it's not working. We're not always the best judge of how we've gone.

Winners and Losers

Towards the end of 2010 things were looking a little grim. I had three children to feed and no-one seemed to want to employ me. I started to get depressed about the state of affairs and even considered what else I could do to earn money. I was being selfish, earning a pittance doing what I wanted to do, when there were other human beings that I was responsible for. It was time to grow up and get a real job and feed my family.

I had to constantly remind myself that even though the work wasn't exactly flowing, I was teaching my children to do what they love and that was a very worthwhile example to set before them. However, although I could see the force of the argument intellectually, I still felt guilty. And useless and depressed.

Being unemployed is an unavoidable part of being an actor. Unless you're unbelievably lucky, you won't get a sequence of jobs, one after the other, like a succession of trams adhering to a schedule. It's more likely to be nothing for six months and then suddenly three come at once. Or, even more likely, nothing for a year, then a tram appears round the corner, stops before it gets to you, waits for a bit and then reverses back around the corner and disappears.

Unemployment is, obviously, very hard economically, but it's almost harder mentally. It's very, very easy to start doubting yourself.

You do need to keep telling yourself that these feelings are often inevitable but not any real reflection of the state of affairs. And you won't get any help from outside. This is not an industry where you get a lot of feedback. Except in the odd review. And then it's not always positive.

The other way to keep yourself going is do something. Fix something round the house, start to write a play, or a song. Get together with some friends and do scenes together. You'll often find that action of whatever sort tends to stir things up and something happens.

So, I was going through one such period of idleness. The children's constant and thoughtless demands for food and new shoes were becoming more and more difficult to satisfy. And then I got a call from my agent.

'They want you for a new TV series. Regular role. It's called *Winners and Losers*.'

Winners and Losers was going to be a family 'dramedy' centred around four girls who bond at school and then continue the relationship later on in life. The role was the father of one of the girls. Denise Scott had already been cast as the mother. Denise was and is one of Australia's most beloved and funny comedians. I knew her to say hello to but had never worked with her before. Melissa Bergland would be playing our daughter, the mercurial and outspoken Jenny Gross.

This was an extraordinary stroke of luck. I could feed the children real food. I could pay some bills and get rid of some debts. I didn't need to get another job. I was worthwhile and wanted. The wolf at the door slunk away. The sun came out. Et cetera.

Then a second call.

'They just want to see you and Denise together.'

'Why? Is it an audition? I thought it was an offer.'

'Yes, of course, but they just want to check how you look together. Don't worry about it.'

'But what if we don't look good together?'

'I'm sure that won't happen. Tuesday at ten good for you?'

The wolf reappeared and the sun went behind a cloud. This was very stressful. Denise was already cast, so it seemed to be a case of whether I looked believable as her husband. I turned up to the non-audition. Denise was there waiting. She said hello. I hoped we seemed a natural fit to the entire Channel 7 management who seemed to be there. I tried to be compatible. I said hello back. So far so good.

Once we were miked up and standing in front of the camera, with the director and producer and the rest of the assembled throng standing round looking at us expectantly, Denise turned and looked at me.

'Oh my God, you're so tall!'

Denise is a giant in Australian comedy. She's not quite so large physically. Not that she's short. She's ... I'm getting myself into trouble here. But she was right, next to each other we did seem slightly different species, although this was not what I wanted her to say. Anyway, no matter, perhaps no-one else had heard.

'You are tall aren't you Francis?' said the producer.

F... it.

'How old are you?' Denise continued.

'I'm 48.'

'Oh, Jesus that's young!'

Thanks Denise. And my dream of not becoming my family's first bankrupt went sailing off into the distance.

I smiled unhappily and shuffled my feet.

'Can you just talk to each other?' came the direction.

I was too stunned at this moment to do anything but contemplate how the only thing greater than the difference in our height was apparently the difference in our ages. (Although if truth be told, the gap is insignificant.) Nothing came to mind.

There was an awkward silence.

Denise came to the rescue.

'You know those letters we get from AMP? What are they?'

I rallied and we were off.

And they must have been convinced because a few days later I was signing a contract and shooting began.

Denise turned out to be a gift to an actor, lovely to work with, a pleasure to be with, and an inexhaustible supply of anecdote in the green room.

The Film Set

I was now on the other side of TV drama, a regular member of the cast, part of the family rather than a tense and nervous guest. I was getting a regular salary for the first time since my days at Magpie. It was absolutely wonderful. And I started to really learn the TV ropes.

The first thing I needed to learn was how to cope with the chaos of the set. It's almost unnecessary to point out that a film set is a busy place. But it is. There are upwards of 50 people working on the set at any one time and the sense of constant activity can be very tiring. And being on a set just about every day for months is completely exhausting.

The temptation is to absorb it. To be part of it. To stand around and chat and let the energy of the workspace infect you. And a lot of people do that. I found it too debilitating in the long run. I would deal with it by closing myself off from the activity, just to protect myself and conserve energy. I would find a corner to sit in and go there between takes. Or I'd go to the toilet. Or if there was more time, I'd go to the green room. Someone would have to come and get me when I was needed on set, but, in my mind at least, that inconvenience was a small price to pay for a refreshed and focused actor.

The exhaustion you feel after a day's shooting is unlike any other tiredness I've ever felt. It's not a physical tiredness so much as metaphysical, spiritual even. Primitive tribes often are wary of being photographed, so the myth goes, because they feel the photo is capturing their soul. And perhaps there's something in that. The constant reproduction of your image on camera is slowly and irreparably destroying your essence.

The best explanation I've heard comes from Shaun Micallef.

As he puts it, in theatre, you rehearse for four weeks. You're making the arrows and stringing the bow and practising aiming.

Then the show comes and every night you point the bow in the right direction, release the string and off flies the arrow. The show is the release of all the work you've done.

In TV, you're constantly being made to aim and pull the string back but you're never allowed to really let it go. You're always doing little bits, the wide shot, someone else's close-up and you do it over and over again. And you're constantly having to wait: for the lighting to be set, for the make-up and costume people to check you, for the other scene to finish so you can do yours. And it's this constant tension of holding the string back without the concomitant relief of being able to let the arrow really fly which causes the exhaustion.

Screen Acting

In one sense, acting for screen is a game where you attempt to act while the whole crew tries to prevent you. You may have a good sense of the scene, and the set may be extremely realistic, even to the extent of having real water coming out of the taps in the sink, but there are 50 people and several cameras only three feet away.

You try to concentrate before a take, but you'll have a swarm of people tugging at you and distracting you, wardrobe will be adjusting your costume, sound will be fiddling with your microphone, the make-up department will want to do something to your face, and the art department will be handing you the casserole dish you have to fling out of the window.

You have to do the same scene over and over again. You have to stop at your mark, which is a bit of tape on the ground, without looking at it; and you have to remember that when you did the wide shot, you picked up your cup on your first line and took a sip after your second and you need to copy that exactly. You may have to act to a small bit of tape attached to the camera stand if it's your close-up and there's no room for the other actors to stand. ***In short, absolutely everything is conspiring to prevent you from acting.*** And that's the real challenge of the film set.

All of which does lead me to the vexed issue of film acting versus stage acting. Or rather the difference between them. And there is no difference. ***Acting is the same basic thing whether you're pretending to be the King of England on stage or Jarrod Niceguy on a TV set.*** The thought processes, the awareness of your circumstances, the work you do to connect emotionally to the situation and the text are all the same no matter whether you're on stage in a 500 seat theatre or freezing your body parts off on a hill at 6:00 a.m. with a camera pointed up your nose and a boom operator fiddling with your trousers.

There are technical differences of course. And there are courses and books about screen acting that will stress these things and tell you to be aware of the size of the shot, and where the light is and what your continuity is, and they're absolutely right, but at the end of the day ultimately it's about being sensible. There's no qualitative difference between the two forms of acting, you just need to be aware of and sensible about the technical requirements and what's going on around you. Don't gesticulate wildly if it's a very close close-up. Try to repeat the same action for take two. If you notice an enormous shadow on your co-actor's face, it might be you that's causing it.

Being sensible.

And I'll go further – all of these many books on acting will tell you how extremely crucial it is that you keep an eye on your own continuity. That you get good at hitting your mark. That you don't overlap your lines with your co-actor's so editing is easier. All estimable things to aim for.

But. At the end of the day this is just making other peoples' lives easier at the expense of your own.

Your main concern is your own performance, not continuity or your co-actor's light or the size of the shot. You're hired to present a character on screen, not to get it in one take. The audience won't know how many takes you took, the only thing they'll be aware of is how powerful or moving or truthful your performance is and how effective the character is in the story. No-one ever got cast because they were good at hitting their mark.

And all the other technical stuff will get taken care of.

If you make a mistake with your continuity, someone with a stopwatch and headphones and a large folder containing a heavily annotated script will emerge from the shadows and tell you that you need to pick up the cup a line later. If you don't hit your mark or you cast a shadow over another actor, you'll do another take. Big deal. If you overlap your line with the other guy's line, well, while it may make the editor's life more difficult, that's their problem. You're actually representing real life – people interrupt and overlap all the time. (You may be told not to overlap and then you should of course, obey, but be aware that the truth of the scene is being sacrificed for convenience.) All that extraneous stuff will be sorted out.

So concentrate on your own shit. On listening, on being in the moment, on what your character wants and has to do. I'm not saying you should ignore everything except your own performance. You don't want to irritate the crew. And being efficient and hitting your mark and getting it in one take means you won't still be there at 7:00 p.m. Obviously try to be sensible and help. But focus on what you're there to do.

And you have rights too. If a mosquito coughs on Mars, the sound department will insist on another take and if the shadow of the boom can vaguely be seen in the window for half a nanosecond, then you'll do the whole thing again. And then after six takes, when the lighting is right and the sound clear and the continuity perfect but your performance is not what you wanted it to be, because you've had to do it over and over again, the pressure to move on is enormous. Better a technically perfect shot with a weak performance than a good performance where a dog barks in the background. And it's difficult to overcome this mindset. Everyone else wants to move on, you're inevitably half an hour behind schedule, the crew is already moving the cameras. So to say 'Could I please have another take?' is a big thing.

But if you want another take, ask for it. No-one's going to ask for it for you and it'll be you with the egg on your face when the thing goes to air. And you have an absolute right to do that, just as the DOP has the right to ask for another take because they can see the boom in shot. And they will always give it to you if you ask.

So remember: you're responsible for your performance. Above all else.

The Grosses

As Brian Gross (my character on *Winners and Losers*), I had three grown-up children. As Francis Greenslade I had three young children. And again, my mother was right. Damn it. I knew instinctively how to relate to my TV family because I had a real life family at home.

The issue of how one's personal life affects or is used to help one's performance is a very large can of worms. Most acting methods or theories are really quite similar. They might take a slightly different approach or see things from a different viewpoint but basically the same principles can be found everywhere. Given circumstances, Actions, Obstacles, Objectives, and so on.

Where they all diverge slightly tends to be over this issue of how to turn the raw matter of our lived experience into performance. At one end of the spectrum, you find the 'it's all in the script' brigade. And at the other end, you have theories that want you to focus on a favourite aunt, explore the emotions associated with her death, have a bit of a cathartic breakdown and then transfer your aunt and associated feelings to the chronically ill child in the script. Again, my prejudices are showing. I think, both extremes have their problems.

There's a subtle and indefinable alchemy that gets us from experience to performance. You could call it empathy but that really only gives a label to the issue without explaining it. I never visualised my own children's faces when talking to my TV children, nor did I ever say to myself, 'I got very scared when my real daughter Charlotte got lost in David Jones and I can use that for my feelings about TV daughter Jenny's breast cancer scare.' For one thing adult children and small children are different creatures and parents have different relationships with each. But I *did* know what it was like to love my children and I *did* know what it was like to talk to them and I was very familiar with what it was like to tick them off and make jokes at them and cook them meals.

And this real life knowledge put me in the right ballpark to be able to interact with the actors playing my TV kids, in just the same way that the death of my son Sam had made me understand what it is to be a bereaved parent.

This doesn't mean that childless actors can't play parents. If you're human, you've loved something and wanted to take care of it and that puts you in the ballpark too. But you have to travel a little further to get there. I had a shortcut because I had experiences that were closer to the given circumstances.

Of course, as the filming went on, we all became closer. I became very fond of Melissa and Sarah and Jack, who were playing my kids, and Denise and I started treating them a little bit like our children, which wasn't difficult after all – they were a good deal younger and we were a discrete group that spent a lot of time together, just like a real family. And that made it easier and easier to play the situation. And the line between actors and characters became more and more blurred. Again, another great shortcut.

Back to Dustin Hoffman. There's a great video of him running a masterclass and directing two actors in a scene from *Good Will Hunting*. It's not working and there's nothing really happening between the male and female actor. Dustin Hoffman asks the girl if she's in love. 'Yes', she says. He then turns to the boy. 'Did you feel a bit jealous when she said that?' And the boy nods.

And suddenly there's tension in the room. And the possibility of romance, love, sex, whatever, between the two *actors* is there. And it's real. So they do the scene again, and it works. Because they were put in a situation where they had to consider themselves as an actual real couple. Real life meets the script.

It's a very powerful example of how, as I've said before, there's no difference between the feelings you really have and the feelings you need to have on stage.

And just as everyone is different, so everyone's personal method is slightly different and what works for some may not work for others. A lot of actors will consciously use images and memories from their past that carry certain emotions to help them in scenes.

I always feel, however, that I'm taking myself away from my given circumstances if I do that and that the sorrow at the loss of a friend, however beloved, is qualitatively different from the sorrow you feel when your child dies. And that consequently you're fudging matters a bit. It's not that simple. But again, whatever gets you through the night. A lot of actors actively and directly use real life experience. And at the end of the day, there's not really a lot of difference between what they do and what I try to do.

It all comes down to apprehension. Or comprehension. Empathy.

I understand the scenario implicitly because I've lived through something similar. Or I've had similar emotions and similar relations. And / or I've done a hell of a lot of imaginative work and I've got a really detailed backstory.

Of course sometimes backstories can let you down. When we started on *Winners and Losers* the writers gave us potted histories of our characters. Mine involved being raised by my father after my mother died. This was extremely helpful, and I decided that Brian Gross was a man who had never had a proper family and was supremely happy in the middle of the one he had created. No angst, no unfulfilled ambition. He had always wanted a family and now he had one. Perfect.

And then we got renewed for a second series and then a third and these things got forgotten and suddenly one day there was a knock on the door and my mother appeared. She's been living in Bendigo all this time. Not dead. And not assumed dead. And lovely to meet her.

But the backstory got quietly binned.

Time and Other Issues

It's nearly always the case that filming TV and film will be done out of order, all the scenes on the spaceship will be filmed on the same day and all those in the slime pit on another as the cost of spaceships and slime pits mounts up if you're constantly hiring them. This means that it's up to the actor to really be on top of where they are in the scheme of things. If you enter having come from the doctor's where you received bad news, you'll do the scene differently than if it's two days earlier and you haven't started coughing yet.

Winners and Losers was particularly complicated. There were six seasons and each was about 26 episodes. We filmed them in 'blocks'. Each block was two episodes filmed over thirteen days. At any one point we would be filming two different episodes, rehearsing for the two to come, adding in dialogue in a recording studio for the two we'd just filmed, and reading scripts for the two after the two to come. It was very hard to keep track of the plot. Characters seemed to be breaking up before they'd got together, falling off the wagon before they'd got on it, and appearing in people's houses after they'd died.

It was perhaps a little easier for Denise and I. As the drama centred around the four girls, we were always slightly on the periphery. Most of our scenes were inside the Gross household and often the only variation seemed to be which one of us was going to be peeling the carrots. Whoever was supplying fresh produce to the *Winners and Losers* art department was making out like a bandit.

One of our directors, Declan Eames, would make the extremely confusing *Winners and Losers* universe very simple by going through everyone's journey before we filmed the scene. 'Jenny, you've come home from work; Denise, you've been cooking all day for this dinner party; and Francis, you fell asleep on the toilet and have only just woken up.' It was a simple and unremarkable thing to do perhaps but it made filming much easier. It's a good habit to get into, to remind yourself what's just happened.

One of the biggest challenges was finding the energy at 5:00 p.m., peeling carrots yet again, doing a fifth take and still being fresh and in the moment and maintaining the fiction that this is the first time you've ever done this and you have no idea what's going to happen next.

How do you manage to be in the moment when you know what's going to happen? ***How do you surprise yourself?***

This is the acting paradox. I know what's going to happen. I've learnt the lines and I know the moves and we've rehearsed the scene. If I'm filming something, then I may have already done it several times. If I'm doing a play, then I did this last night and the night before and the night before. And I have to know the moves and lines or we couldn't do the scene or the play. ***But the character has no idea what's about to happen.***

How do I reconcile my knowledge with the character's ignorance and pretend not to know what's about to happen?

I discovered that if I focused on my expectations then this problem was at least partially solved. I ask Denise as Trish Gross to pass the carrot peeler, but she is cross with me and doesn't. We've already shot the wide and her close-up and the two-shot, and now it's my single. How do I keep on reacting truthfully when I've done this several times already?

Well, if I ask her to pass me something, my expectation is that she will, so if I focus on the expected outcome of her picking up the peeler and putting it into my hand, it's much easier to react when the expectation isn't met. I'm having to deal with the tiny shock of image not coinciding with reality. Something has happened that I wasn't expecting. And I have to take that fact in before I can react to it.

This is particularly helpful with entrances. The books will tell you to think about where you've been and why you are entering. Which is helpful – those circumstances will alter how you enter.

But once that work is done, focusing on your expectation of what you will see when you do come in will help you keep it fresh. The situation you're entering will quite often not be what you expect and the job of assimilating the true situation somehow takes you off the railway track of the way you've been doing the scene and puts you smack bang into the moment.

What do you expect to see when you come in? What do you expect the other character to say?

Preparing for spontaneity.

One of the most awkward things about film acting is having the camera hold on you at the end of the scene. The director will always leave the camera on you longer than necessary, just in case you give him something extra, but it can be very hard to be natural and truthful when the scene's finished and the lines have all been spoken and all there is left is a close-up of you, trying not to mug but at the same time trying to give the director something memorable. It's a real soapie technique and it can look really corny.

A good way of dealing with this is to imagine how this scene would continue. In life, scenes don't actually end. It's just an artificial boundary set up by the writer. People may leave the room but we still go on. We deal with the aftermath of what's just happened or we move on to the next thing but there's always something that happens next. What is it?

If you focus on what's next, you won't feel so exposed at the end of the scene. Don't fixate on finishing or ending something that wouldn't have a natural ending in real life.

We spent a lot of time sitting down to meals. The writers loved it as it was an easy way of getting the whole family and assorted hangers-on in the one scene, but the crew hated it as it meant there were at least five people in the scene and sometimes more than ten, and this meant a lot of coverage as every character had to have their own shot and sometimes a two-shot with another character as well. The scenes were very static and would take hours to shoot.

It also brought the issue of eating food on screen front and centre. Catering on a TV show is always very good and very generous. We'd often forget we had a meal scene and turn up on set after lunch to find another lunch waiting for us. Or worse, we'd turn up after breakfast to find the first scene of the day involved spaghetti bolognaise. Some actors dealt with this by not eating at all. Taking the fork out of their mouth just before they spoke as if they had just taken a bite. And some would eat but they would cut their food up into miniscule portions and just eat a small slice of carrot or a few peas.

I always felt this was a mistake. There's nothing more satisfying than seeing actors hoe into food on screen. It's another form of committing to the action. You're in a restaurant or at the dinner table at home, so presumably you're there because you're hungry. Taking tiny little bites of something is copping out. And it's not truthful, no-one does that. ***If you're going to eat, then really eat.*** And bugger the calories.

Winners and Losers was a very successful show and ran for five seasons. It meant that for five years I had something like full-time work. It felt like an extraordinary luxury to have money put into my account every week but, of course, as time went on, I just got used to it and when suddenly it stopped it came as a bit of a shock.

An actor's life, even with the most careful planning, is always a bit feast or famine. Tonight we get takeaway, tomorrow we sit in the dark to save electricity.

Mad as Hell

When *Winners and Losers* finally finished up, I was unemployed again. I grew a beard. I became quite attached to it. Obviously. The rest of the family were divided about its merits. They had not yet exhausted the fertile topic of the deficiencies in my personal appearance when Shaun rang. He had a new ABC show about to start, *Mad as Hell*, and he wanted me to be in it. It was a comic look at what was going on in politics in Australia that week. Roz Hammond, Emily Taheny, Tosh Greenslade (no relation), and later Stephen Hall formed the rest of the cast. Veronica Milson left us after the fourth series to become a Triple J presenter. We would be playing multiple characters in sketches and interviews.

The beard discussion became moot. It would have to go. If I was to convincingly play many different characters, then they couldn't all have beards, could they? Especially the women. Muted cheers.

But even if I had only been playing one character I think it would still have had to go. Beards are strange things. Or rather, they're not, they're just a bit boring. They have a slightly stultifying effect. They might give gravitas but they take away a lot of flexibility. Perhaps because they act as a bit of a mask. They obscure part of the face and that limits us somehow. Or makes us less vulnerable.

But over and above that they're really not right for comedy. The beard is an anti-comic device. There's something about it that is just not suited to the ancient art of getting laughs. In fact, when you think about it, there are very few, if any, comedians or comic actors that actually have beards.

Insert thinking time here.

Can't think of any, can you?

Billy Connolly perhaps. But that's a pretty extreme beard and it suits his unkempt Scottish persona. So unless you're aiming for a sort of comic Wild Man of Borneo look in your comedy, eschew the beard.

But at the time of writing I'm working on *Shakespeare in Love* for the MTC. A large cast all dressed in Elizabethan costumes and most with luxuriant beards and moustaches. And audiences are laughing their heads off. So there's always exceptions.

Shaun came to *Mad as Hell* straight from another news parody, SBS's *Newstopia*. It was more international in scope than *Mad as Hell* but necessarily some elements of the first show bled into the second. One such item was the vox pops segment where the cast would pretend to be members of the general public interviewed in the street. These were played quite straight in *Newstopia*. No 'characters', just normal people. The cast as themselves almost. I didn't want to just play it straight, so when it came to my turn to do one of these little pieces to camera, I asked Karchi, Shaun's make-up artist, to make me look a little kooky. He gave me luxuriant sideburns. Gail, in charge of wardrobe, gave me a pair of interesting looking glasses, a shirt and tie and a jacket with leather elbow patches. When I looked in the mirror the man who appeared seemed to be offended about something. And when he spoke it came out as a furious tirade. At the top of his voice. I asked the art department for a small plastic bag with a very small carton of milk inside. I wanted to suggest that his milk requirements were minimal and that therefore he was single. Very much so. Again, the power of the prop.

He got christened Larry Sideburns, somewhat unoriginally, and as far as the vox pops went he was quite an effective character. Quite a limited character too, as all he was able to do was fulminate at the top of his voice. But I was pleased with him because he came into being almost despite me and he told me how to play him. Or rather it became obvious how to play him once I saw him in the mirror. Magpie's trance mask work in another form.

This was the really exciting part of *Mad as Hell*, creating characters. A quick discussion with make-up and wardrobe, a quick look in the mirror and we're off. And if they worked, the writers would bring them back and they'd become regular characters. Later this character creation became more difficult as the writers tended to write for existing characters, meaning there was less opportunity for new ones. I also discovered that often the interviews worked better straight. Trying to wedge an interesting character into 30 seconds or a minute seemed wrong and it was better to just say the lines and get the gag out properly. Another example of William H. Macy's point about 'just doing the part' and not trying to make something of it.

Larry became a regular. But I never felt he worked on screen. He was more amusing live – there was something quite funny about his refusal to obey the normal conventions of conversational volume. On screen, his sound level was always adjusted by the sound department and then later by the editing department so that it was bearable. Which is understandable. However, he only worked as a character who shouted inappropriately and that never seemed to come across on television. He's a live character, not a TV one, and he's most successful, and happiest, standing on Glen Huntly Rd, Elsternwick, fulminating to an invisible interviewer and making the camera crew laugh.

As the show went on, it developed from *Newstopia*. More and more characters like Larry started to appear and it became quite insane with sketches that involved stuffed zebras or cardinals from the Vatican hitting each other or a man in a badly made octopus suit coming out of a small cupboard to the sound of Toni Basil's 80's hit, *Mickey*.

But it also had its challenges. Being a topical show, it would be written on the Thursday, Friday, Saturday and Sunday, filmed on Tuesday and then it would go out on Wednesday. The cast would start to get scripts coming through on Friday, but they wouldn't be finalised until the Monday. So the preparation time was almost non-existent.

Line learning did actually become quite an issue. There was generally an autocue available, but I never liked to use it if I could avoid it. And even if you did use autocue, you still needed to learn the lines, or at least know them very well.

But it was always better to try to have them off by heart. There's something about the words coming from one's memory that helps truthfulness. It's so close to the process of creating them for the first time. Reading is a completely different thing to acting and I found it very hard to read lines and be the character.

The smallness of our contribution also made things difficult. The show is centred very heavily around Shaun, and on the live night, when we came to film the main part of the show, we would have, on average, two sketches to do for the whole night. But we had to come in and match Shaun's energy. **Sometimes small parts are harder than large parts.** You don't have the luxury of warming up to it, you have to hit the ground running. You've got two minutes screen time, if that, and it has to be right from the word go.

Compounding that was the fact that we had a long day but with very little time allocated to us. We would arrive for a read-through of the script at 12:30 on Tuesday. We would then rehearse in front of camera. This took all afternoon and as a general rule you would get to go through each sketch twice. Then a break for dinner and then into wardrobe and make-up and we'd record the show.

This meant that you'd get one read-through and two goes at your sketch. Over the course of the whole day. Before doing it that night. It became vital to be focused. The crucial thing was to pace yourself and ensure that not only were you using the small amount of rehearsal time properly, but that you didn't lose focus while you were waiting. You could turn off if you had an hour or so, but you needed to be able to turn back on when required.

So on live nights I put myself in a tunnel. At the end of the tunnel was the sketch and the start was being called to go on set. I didn't allow myself to see anything around me. I could only focus on getting the sketch done. And everything else – the warm-up guy, chatting to Shaun, paying attention to what was going on around me on set – was only going to take me out of the tunnel and make it harder to do the sketch.

It made it less fun – *Mad as Hell*'s live night is an entertaining evening. Shaun would talk to the audience, answer their questions and do schtick with the warm-up guy. But I had to remove myself from it. I deliberately put myself into my own world and avoided any sort of banter. And on the occasions when I did give in to the temptation to chat, I found that, inevitably, we had to do more than one take because I lost my lines.

'I can't talk now, I'm pillaging.' The author on location. Mad as Hell. *(Photo: Nikki Hamilton-Cornwall)*

I've been performing Shaun's scripts for over 30 years now. And watching others perform them. They are deceptively difficult to do. The crucial thing to bear in mind is that Shaun doesn't write naturalistic prose. It's heightened language and very stylised. You can't throw the lines away.

Australians are very good at casual, kitchen-sink naturalism. Break up the lines, bring the volume down, toss the words out quickly and casually. But you can't do this with Micallef. The words are their own glory and they need articulation and energy. All the way to the end. They are often ridiculous, provocative, transgressive, poetic and they need to be relished. And there's a rhythm that needs attending to, even if the line is lengthy. ***And you need to keep up the energy of the line all the way to the end.***

And the reason I mention this is that what's true for Shaun's lines is true for Sheridan and Neil Simon and Oscar Wilde. This is high comedy, if you like, and the shape of the language is just as important as the meaning. Australian and American comedy can be very underplayed and we've got out of the habit of giving the lines their full worth. But you can't hang back with Micallef, and doing his stuff is good training for all those other heightened comic styles.

You Got Older

I was asked to be in a play called *You Got Older* written by playwright Clare Barron. A young woman has to confront, well, getting older. Death, life's purpose, family, the lot.

The theatre company was Red Stitch, a small independent company based in Melbourne, run on an oily rag. Often the lower the pay, the worse the resources and the more unknown the cast, the better the work. That was certainly the case with this play. An enthusiastic, ego-less group of actors, whose only thought was how to make the play work, not whether they would look good doing it. It was a lovely thing to be part of.

The play starts with Mae (played by Emily Goddard) and her father (played by me) standing slightly awkwardly in my garden. Talking about peppers.

First scenes are a bugger. There's so much riding on them and so much important information to get across that it's really difficult not to fall into a stagey sort of performance instead of something that's truthful and natural and spontaneous. It always takes the actors a little time to get into the swing of it and so first scenes tend to be slightly 'lacquered'. Artificial. And sometimes even a bit wooden.

The thing to remember is that, just like the end of a scene in a TV drama, the beginning of the play is not really the beginning of anything. It's an artificial starting point because we have to start somewhere. But, like any moment of time, it's actually right in the middle of events. ***There's always something that happened before, and it's helpful to be aware of what that is.***

So in rehearsal we improvised the moment before the first scene and then went into the scene immediately. It made a colossal difference to the way we played it. Much more natural. Less stagey. And it all made a bit more sense.

Once we were doing it in front of an audience, we would stand in the wings, waiting to go on at the top of the show and go through a sort of whispered impro of the moments immediately preceding the start of the play. This made it feel less like a beginning and more like something that was already in the process of happening.

> MAE: Hi Dad.
> FATHER: Mae! You made it.
> MAE: Yeah.
> FATHER: You should have told me! I would have picked you up from the bus.
> MAE: I wanted to walk. How are you?
> FATHER: Good. Good. You're looking well.
> MAE: Yeah.
> *Pause.*
> FATHER: Come and look at the garden. I want to show you the peppers.

Or words to that effect.

And then the house lights would go out and the music would come on, and we'd make our entrance and **continue the action. Rather than start it.**

We did a lot of improvisation during rehearsals. Most of it to establish Mae's family history. The actors playing my children improvised a family conversation around my hospital bed. They improvised a family wedding. My youngest daughter came out to me. I started to develop a twitch every time Brett Cousins, our director, even mentioned the word 'impro'. However, it was extremely beneficial. We gave ourselves an enormous amount of family history and, by the time the audience got to see it, we all had the same finely detailed story in our heads and it gave the family scenes a real truth. If I say so myself.

It helped me at the end of the play too. In the penultimate scene, my character rings Mae to tell her that (spoiler) my cancer has come back and I don't have long to live. By the end of the conversation we are both in tears.

I would stand in the wings just before the scene, trying to work myself up into the requisite emotional state to tell my daughter that I was going to die. And surprisingly, because of the work we had done, just the thought of having to tell my children I didn't have long to live and how they would react, was enough to make me very teary. And this is my stage children, mind, not my real ones. The work that we'd done creating a shared history was so effective that just extrapolating from the world we'd created was enough to generate the emotional state I needed to do the scene.

As I say, I know actors often use their own history to generate emotion. And good on them. But if you've created your world well enough, you really don't need to.

Just before this scene, while everything is still fine, Mae and her father see deer outside the kitchen window. It's a lovely moment of joyous stillness.

I had no problem visualising these deer at all and I realised how far I'd come in 30 years from the clarinet-torturing youth attempting to imagine dead harp seals.

If you just keep plugging away, the years pass and you suddenly realise that you've come a long way, you can do things that you wouldn't have been able to even contemplate doing at the beginning, and you have achieved, dare I say it, competence. It's hard to see one's improvement as an actor as it happens. It's really only time that does it for you.

The author imagines deer living more successfully than he imagined seals dying. With Emily Goddard in You Got Older. *Red Stitch. (Photo: Jodie Hutchinson)*

The Odd Couple

Shaun was approached by the MTC to see if he wanted to do anything for them. He asked me if I would do Neil Simon's *The Odd Couple* with him. I jumped at the chance. *The Odd Couple* is a classic. Two mismatched friends share a house, one obsessively neat, the other a slob. The story of any share house really. It's very funny but also quite moving. Two quite conservative men, dumped by their wives and having to find themselves again. It's had a very long and varied life. It's been a play, a film and several TV series. It was rewritten for a female cast, for an African American cast, and Simon even wrote a sequel, *The Odd Couple 2*. It is, without a doubt, a classic.

We initially had some difficulty allocating the two main roles. Our first idea was to swap them, alternating every week. Peter Houghton, who was to direct, wisely squashed that idea. Eventually we met in a small room at the MTC and read through the play twice, taking turns to play Felix, the obsessively neat neurotic, and Oscar, the slovenly grouch. When we finished, we turned to Peter, who had a look of slight consternation.

'I think you're both Felix.'

He was right. Over the years Shaun and I have probably developed a similar comic delivery. Or at least our comic styles belong to the same universe. And Felix suited both our comic energies. Impasse. In the end, as I've mentioned earlier, I thought I would be happier inhabiting Oscar, and Shaun was quite keen on Felix, so Peter cast us accordingly. And we started rehearsals.

I was now facing the spectre of Walter Matthau. The film of *The Odd Couple* is extremely well known and Matthau's performance is really the Ur Oscar. It's difficult to imagine anyone other than Matthau in the role.

I dealt with this by ignoring it. It was only going to make me feel incapable and the worst thing I could do was to try to copy him.

In the end, there were some lines I felt I couldn't help but deliver like Matthau, but I did feel, for good or ill, that both Shaun and I managed to avoid presenting pale imitations of Matthau and Jack Lemmon's Felix. Or, as Peter said later, we completely obliterated them.

Of course, there were some who came expecting a version of the film and they were never going to be happy.

I now had to deal with the fact that I wasn't really a good fit for Oscar. I remember chatting to an actor after a show.

'I see you're doing *The Odd Couple*?'

'Yes.'

'And you'd be …', and a look of puzzlement came over his face, not unlike that of a colour-blind person trying to do a Rubik's cube, 'Felix?'

And I could understand his bewilderment. If I was casting myself I'd probably cast me as Felix. I don't really have Oscar's solidity.

Peter spent some time on this during rehearsals. 'You, Francis, live in your head. You've got to find some heaviness. You're such a forward, quick actor. You're always on the balls of your feet and Oscar is not.'

This was quite confronting. The acting fraternity is always very careful not to comment on each other's work except in very positive terms, so to hear my acting analysed was something I'd never experienced.

In retrospect I'm very grateful. The whole process of learning to act runs parallel to the process of learning who we are. The greater the self-knowledge, the better the actor. And Peter gave me a glimpse of myself. If this journey to self-knowledge is a lifelong walk, he had driven past in his car, stopped and given me a lift down the road a little. Contorted metaphor. Apologies.

And he was right. I do live in my head. I am firmly in the Richard Briers rapid-fire comic delivery camp as opposed to the Steve Wright one. Google them. And my walk and stance tend to be a little unanchored. I'm a low-status specialist too. And Oscar isn't low status. Although Felix is.

So I had some work to do. I needed to ground myself more. Achieve a heaviness. I focused on my walk. As I've said, this is often my point of departure for character. If I can find the character's walk, then I can move around like him and I'm more than halfway there.

I needed to make my walk heavier and more substantial. And here we move into perhaps slightly distasteful territory. Apologies in advance. Anyone of a delicate disposition is encouraged to move on to the next chapter.

I decided that Oscar had an enormous penis.* And this, I hoped, would alter my walk and give it that heaviness. But I didn't feel it was enough to just imagine it. I needed to have one. I had no idea, however, how one would acquire such an object. I considered visiting a sex shop and asking for an artificial penis. The possibility of being seen by someone who knew me put the kybosh on that idea. And did they have fitting rooms where you tried these things on? It was too much to deal with. I googled artificial penises for sale online, but they all seemed so anatomical. I really didn't need one with veins. And so I decided to make one myself. After several abortive textile-based experiments, I settled on a piece of red flannel. I wrapped it around my own membrum virile and it gave me length and width. I bought some medical tape to attach it. A design flaw became evident. It proved impossible to stick the thing on without coming into contact with pubic hair which made it then impossible to remove without discomfort. But all in the cause of art.

One day when I had the house to myself I took out my device and attached it. I tried walking. Success. It gave me a completely different gait with a heavier energy but also, it seemed, a more positive one. And Oscar, even though he can be a grouch, is a sociable and cheery thing when his routine isn't destroyed. In fact, human contact is the thing he craves most.

But the most crucial thing was that it became organic. It wasn't just something I had intellectually foisted upon myself. It entered my bones and became part of the character. It felt right. And when I took the thing off and walked around, I could recreate the feeling and thus the walk. Happiness. Say that carefully.

---

* Author's penis is of a satisfactory size.

I had several goes at this, just walking round the house and getting used to the feel of the thing. Once I was ready, I even took it into rehearsals. This proved to be not a good idea. I was so terrified it would fall off, and so unable to think of a way of explaining to the rest of the cast why a piece of red flannel with tape attached to it had fallen down my trouser leg, that I spent the first half hour of rehearsals in such a state of rigid self-absorption that I had to admit defeat and go to the toilet and take it off. In the long run it didn't matter. I only had to wear it every once in a while, just to remind myself of what it felt like. To get a recharge, so to speak.

A few days after I had started wearing it, Peter came up to me.

'You've really got the character now, Francis, well done.'

I didn't tell him how.

I was obviously taking on more of Oscar the slob than an impressive packed lunch because I was leaving medical tape, with what was obviously pubic hair still attached to it, on the floor of the bathroom when I removed the device in question.

One night Louise was in an unusually quiet and sombre mood. And when we were by ourselves in bed, she said, 'I don't know what you're doing, but could you not leave bits of tape in the bathroom?'

I said I wouldn't.

'Do you want to know what it's for?'

There was a pause. I'm not sure what images were passing through her head.

'Yes.'

I explained. Another pause. This one was easier to read. It went from 'Does he expect me to believe that?' through to 'It *is* the sort of thing he would do' alighting briefly on 'Thank God it's only that' before finishing up on 'You f...... idiot.'

There was no doubt about the last thought, however, because if memory serves me correctly, she vocalised it.

After the season I asked her whether she had noticed anything different in my walk on stage.

'I'd completely forgotten about that. No. I didn't.'

I was slightly disappointed, but in the end it made a difference to me and to the character. And if Louise didn't notice it, then perhaps it's because it just seemed normal.

I started rehearsals preoccupied by Oscar's untidiness. I was worried that it wasn't present enough. Felix's tidiness features throughout the play but after the first scene in Act 1 Simon seems to completely forget about Oscar. I started looking for places to be untidy in the second half of the play.

Once we started to put the scenes together, however, I realised that I was obsessing for no good reason. Oscar's untidiness is set up very clearly in the first few pages: he wipes his hands on Roy's jacket and uses a sandwich to mop up some spilt beer. Once that's done, there's no need to advert to it any more; in fact, it's a waste of effort. We all know Oscar's a slob, so why keep on telling us? You're just wasting words you could be using for better things, like advancing the plot.

It's a useful lesson for character. **Once you've established something – untidiness, a cold, whatever little idiosyncrasy, invented or prescribed that your character may have – there's absolutely no need to keep establishing it.** It just becomes empty, unnecessary, irritating repetition. Do it a few times at the beginning and then forget about it. Unless it's part of the action.

Neil Simon is a very talky playwright. Characters stand on stage and say amusing things to each other. That's not to say that there's no action, but there's a hell of a lot of chat. I found myself doing less and less during rehearsals and concentrating on listening more and more. There didn't seem to be any reason to do anything except listen and if I did find some bit of business it just seemed to distract from what was being said. And the more the play advanced and the more our two characters started to get a little hot under the collar, the more I felt I had to just stand there and listen.

The higher the stakes, the more you need to focus on your interlocutor, because the more important their words are.

And as a corollary to that, if you do take the focus off what the other person is saying by some bit of business, then you're in effect saying to the audience, 'Don't worry about this bit, it's not important. Watch me adjust my tie instead'. And they will.

Halfway through rehearsals I got stuck on a line and I couldn't get off. The Pigeon sisters, who live in an upstairs apartment, have been invited for dinner and Oscar is getting frisky. The conversation turns to how hot it is in the girls' apartment.

Here's the exchange:

> CECILY: Last night was so bad Gwen and I sat there in nature's own cooling ourselves in front of the open frig. Can you imagine such a thing?
>
> OSCAR: Er, I'm working on it.

For some reason I couldn't get it. I tried it with a pause in the middle of the line. I tried it without a pause, I cut the 'Er', I put it back in, I made it an 'Um' but nothing seemed to work. Peter had a go. Shaun had a go. Michala and Christie, playing the girls, tried the line. This was now getting tedious. And eventually we all gave up and it remained unsolved.

As soon as I got in front of an audience, however, everything became clear. I discovered that if I turned to the audience and then said the line, I got a huge laugh. And any other way of doing it seemed wrong.

And there were several other moments in the play that straightened themselves out as soon as we did them to an audience.

Sometimes if a moment isn't working, it's OK to leave it till you get into the theatre. ***The audience will teach you how to do the play.***

Several times, the solution was just that simple – look to the audience. Felix says he's going to tell Oscar a few home truths. He's furious, but although it seems like it's going to be critical, all he says are nice things.

> FELIX: Alright I warned you … You're a wonderful guy, Oscar. You've done everything for me. If it weren't for you, I don't know what would've happened to me. You took me in here, gave me a place to live and something to live for. I'll never forget you for that. You're tops with me Oscar.
>
> OSCAR: If I've just been told off, I think I may have missed it.

Again, the audience taught me that if I just looked at them before my line there was another huge laugh, and if I was lucky, I could get a laugh after the line as well. I don't know how I realised that was what the audience wanted. They asked for the look, somehow. And somehow I realised they were asking for it. It's breaking the fourth wall slightly. A gesture of complicity. It said 'Get a load of him' and they loved it.

Shaun Micallef suggesting to the author an alternative to a bit of red cloth with tape on it. The Odd Couple, MTC. *(Photo: Jeff Busby)*

It was a revelation to me that they were actually on my side. **The audience wanted to like me.** And I didn't need to be scared of them (which I had been ever since Grade 2, if I'm honest with myself).

And that I could play with them. I had known this intellectually but this was a more visceral understanding of their willingness to come towards me. An advanced stage of my career to realise this, but better late than never.

In the second act, Felix moves in with Oscar and starts making the house neat. With negative consequences for the poker game that's going on. At last he stops cleaning and sits down to play.

OSCAR: I can't believe it. We're going to play cards again ... It's up to Roy. Roy, baby, what are you gonna do?
ROY: I'm going to get in a cab and go to Central Park. If I don't get some fresh air, you got yourself a dead accountant.

During the beginning of the run, Roy's first line, 'I'm going to get in a cab and go to Central Park' always got a laugh, but halfway through the run, it disappeared. I couldn't work out why. Then I realised that one of the other cast members always adjusted his chair just before his line. Which distracted the audience.

It always takes a little bit of an effort to follow dialogue, but looking at things takes virtually none at all and the audience's attention will always go to the visual, to the detriment of the aural. The eyes before the ears.

If you invent business then you need to be absolutely sure it's contributing to what's happening at that moment. If you're not speaking, then quite probably someone else is and they need the focus, not you. You need to be very clear why you are taking that focus and also sure that it's to the benefit of the scene, rather than the benefit of you.

Generally, your action is to listen. Someone is saying something, probably to you. You're going to respond to it when they've finished talking. **So listen. Really listen. You've never heard this before. And you're going to be changed by what they say.**

What's more your attention on them will focus the audience's attention on them too.

Audiences can't be relied on to concentrate all the way through. Their attention wanders. To the set, to an actor not speaking, to the person sitting next to them. If an audience member looks at an actor and that actor is focused on the speaker, then the audience member will look back at the speaker. Job well done. If that actor is doing something, or looking somewhere else, however, the audience member will immediately look at what he or she is doing or where they're looking, and then they miss what's really happening. Anyone who was looking at me during that matinee of *Accidental Death of an Anarchist* would have noticed me staring into the audience and would have looked round to see what I was looking at. Perhaps that's what Berkoff was doing. My job was to feed into the action, to be in the moment, no matter how difficult, and to focus attention back to the main event.

What can I say, I was young and stupid.

Think of yourself and everyone else on stage as forming one of those dish-shaped reflective mirror things. Your job is to focus the audience's attention into the centre, to who's speaking.

The Odd Couple turned out to be one of the most financially successful shows the MTC had ever produced. Thanks mainly to the presence of Shaun. It's always slightly deflating to perform to less than full houses, but with *The Odd Couple* we never had to. It was quite extraordinary to go out every night to a completely packed out theatre. We got used to it, of course. There was one matinee that was only two-thirds full and I remember feeling quite aggrieved that we had to do the show to such an paltry audience.

Reviews

Some actors say, 'I never read reviews.' I used to wish that I had the self-restraint not to, but I couldn't help myself. I always wanted to know what the reviewer thought.

It was, curiously enough, never a positive experience. If the review was bad, it made it difficult to continue to perform with positivity and confidence. On the other hand, any positive mention tended to destroy the moment it was referring to: 'Francis excels in the soup-making scene', and the scene was never as good again.

Just like specific praise from a director, compliments tend to alter one's mental circumstances and the change is always for the worse. All in all, it is probably best not to be mentioned at all, although difficult not to feel slightly aggrieved if one isn't.

I was well aware of all of this intellectually but it didn't seem to change my behaviour. I still avidly read the damn things.

Then while I was doing *The Odd Couple*, a review appeared in *The Australian*. It was not particularly glowing. The reviewer, who shall remain nameless (Chris Boyd), declared, and I quote:

> Although not an actor of prodigious range, Francis Greenslade projects Oscar's character as effortlessly as he projects his voice.

I didn't know where to begin with this. Apart from the fact that I didn't necessarily agree with his assessment of my versatility, it seemed completely unnecessary to comment on it.

'Francis Greenslade makes a shithouse *Hamlet*. It's lucky for him that he's playing Lear. Which he does quite well, I suppose.'

It was as though the reviewer had decided beforehand to be negative about my performance, and failing to find anything unpleasant to say, had been forced to critique my career as a sort of supplementary slap in the face.

That was the trigger and I've tried to avoid reviews ever since.

It's difficult, I know, but don't read reviews. They are not your friend. Like seeing oneself on screen, anything that adds a self-consciousness to your performance is to be avoided.

Teaching

I was now approaching Don Barker's age but I didn't seem to be receiving any advantage casting-wise. All my contemporaries seemed extremely healthy and very busy. And long may it stay that way, I hasten to add. But one thing that did happen as I got older was that people seemed to assume that I knew what I was doing and asked me to direct.

The first directing job was a student production of *The Golden Age* by Louis Nowra. It's a sprawling, ambitious, lucky-dip of a play with lost tribes and invented languages, music, war, theatre, magic and madness all packed in together. Slightly ambitious for a small drama school.

What struck me most about the experience of directing was the number of decisions I was constantly being asked to make. Designers would show me two identical chairs and ask me to choose the one I wanted, stage managers wanted to know where to put it and actors wanted to know when they should sit on it. And some of these decisions were important. But some were not. I quickly learnt that the important thing was to make a decision and be definite.

'Which hat shall we use, Francis, the green or the brown?'

'The brown, definitely. It's much better. Much browner.'

You could always change your mind later.

'Why is that hat so very brown? It looks awful.'

'You chose it, Francis.'

'Don't we have a green one?'

You need to learn to make your own decisions as an actor. Don't ask the director where you should sit – sit where you think you should and see how that goes. That's what rehearsal is for. I've always found directors are very grateful to actors who make offers. They may have no idea how the scene is supposed to look and you've just rescued them. And if they don't like the offer, then they'll say so. No harm done.

The director has a lot on their mind, they're relying on you to do the character. You're making their job a lot easier if you just do what you want instead of asking what someone else thinks. With the added advantage that you get to create the performance yourself rather than following instructions.

It was at this point, confident that if I could direct it was natural that I could also teach, I rented a small office and attempted to set up a small acting coaching practice.

I was not, initially, a very good teacher. I believe and hope that I have improved but at the beginning, although I could see quite clearly what was needed in a performance or a monologue, I couldn't communicate it.

One student had a habit of always going up in intonation at the end of the sentence. This made her sound monotonous and it became difficult to attend to what she was saying.

I made the mistake of trying to address the symptom.

'You're going up at the end of the line. Can you try going down instead?'

Unsurprisingly this didn't help.

'No, like this.' And I did the line for her. Again, not helpful.

I don't mind directors giving me a line reading occasionally. I'm old and ugly enough not to fall into the trap of just copying their performance. But I think you need to be much more careful with younger actors. They will just end up copying you instead of finding the right way by themselves.

At any rate, I was unable to help this student and I wasn't surprised when she stopped coming to me.

What I *should* have spoken about was why she was doing this and what she needed to focus on to remedy it. Let's see if I can do better now.

'You voice is going up at the end of the line and I think it's because you're not finishing your thought. Could you start the line with only the one thought in your head and then finish it? Then the next thought occurs to you and you say that. There's no need to link the two necessarily.'

And indeed, the more I work with young students the more I come across this. It stems from the idea that if I have eight sentences in my speech, and the second leads on from the first and then leads on to the third, then the temptation is to read them as though I've prepared my speech. That I know what I'm going to say next and so I lead from one sentence to the next. And so my speech becomes a list of thoughts that I've prepared. This produces a constant upward inflection at the end of the thought as a link to the next thought. It's monotonous and unpleasant to listen to for too long. But more importantly, because the character is just rattling off a list, it lowers the stakes and undermines the importance of what the character is saying. The fact that the character is just giving us a list implies that they don't really care about what they're talking about.

It's so important to be absolutely clear about what you're saying and why you're saying it. **And then finish the thought.** Don't give the impression that you're going to continue. People generally don't know what they're going to say after they finish the thing they're saying at the time. So, copy that. You've only got one thing to say at the moment. Don't worry about the next thing, just say what you're saying and finish it. Full stop. Then the upward inflection disappears without you thinking about it. And then, as in real life, the next thing suddenly occurs to you and you start to say that. A new thought. Without, again, any awareness that you're going to say anything after that. **You know what you're going to say, the character doesn't.**

This really gives an impression of a character right in the moment, spontaneously dealing with new thought after new thought. And it brings the audience into the moment too.

This was brought home to me during the shooting of *Mad as Hell*. I found myself standing on a street in suburban Elsternwick holding a chicken under my arm and reciting a list of places the chicken might like to go in the car I had placed at his disposal. I think it's worth printing the Camillo sketch, penned by the great Micallef, in full.

> *Cut to* CAMILLO, *not foreign; in a neat pair of overalls, being interviewed in the street in front of an apartment block in a nice suburb.* CAMILLO *nurses an impressive looking hen.*

CAMILLO: I own this apartment block and Claude here lives in it by himself. He's free to come and go as he pleases. I have a car available to take him to the pictures or the market or to visit friends or go tadpoling or the pub or the races or a concert or paintballing or the optometrist or perhaps go to the aquarium or dancing or a hike or something or skateboarding or to donate blood or do a bit of gargling or go to lunch or check out the new community garden they've put on the roof of that abandoned peanut factory or maybe he might have a court appearance or an appointment with his accountant or church or to buy some clothes or go to the fair – any number of things. I don't want to go into too much detail obviously. I mean, it's his business. My business is getting eggs out of him which is hard enough for him even with all the space he has. I can't imagine what it would be like for him to have to live with other chickens. Ten years I've had him so far and not one egg. But we're easing into it, aren't we boy?

The trick is to recite the list without making it sound like a list. To finish each thought, as I've described above. To search for, and find, each new activity. Camillo has absolutely no idea what he's going to say next, each new activity is a new idea. ***The only thing you're intending to say is what you're currently saying.***

I use this sketch as an exercise for students quite often now and it's surprisingly difficult. But it's a very good way of coming to grips with that idea of the new thought. Of not acting in lists. And of avoiding that dreaded upward inflection.

Another common trap for students was being influenced by the physical appearance of the words on the page.

Most monologues appear in two-dimensional form as a squarish block. As the chicken speech above does. And unconsciously, the young actor reads it as a block, starting at the beginning and just running through it. Without thought. As though each sentence is of the same essence as the one before and the one after it.

The author with Hildegard the chicken. The author in overalls. Mad as Hell. *(Photo: Nikki Hamilton-Cornwall)*

But that's not what happens in real life. And we come back to the idea of the new thought. Usually, each sentence is saying something different. That's why there's a full stop. It comes into being because we think of something else to say. We are trying to explain, or pacify, or contradict, or instruct or accuse, or any number of things, as the good Camillo says. And the sentence after that one is trying to do something different again. And we need to mark those new intentions.

A really helpful technique to mark these new intentions is to think in brackets. And instead of me laboriously describing how that works, let me laboriously demonstrate it for you instead. Let's try it with Shakespeare, partly because if it works for iambic pentameter it'll work for anything, but mainly for reasons of copyright.

Here's the famous ring speech from Shakespeare's *Twelfth Night*. Viola who is disguised as a man, realises that Olivia has fallen in love with her/him after Malvolio, Olivia's servant, gives her a ring that he falsely but unknowingly asserts Viola has given to Olivia. Got that? Excellent.

> VIOLA: I left no ring with her: what means this lady?
> Fortune forbid my outside have not charm'd her!
> She made good view of me; indeed, so much,
> That sure methought her eyes had lost her tongue,
> For she did speak in starts distractedly.
> She loves me, sure; the cunning of her passion
> Invites me in this churlish messenger.
> None of my lord's ring! why, he sent her none.
> I am the man: if it be so, as 'tis,
> Poor lady, she were better love a dream.
> Disguise, I see, thou art a wickedness,
> Wherein the pregnant enemy does much.
> How easy is it for the proper-false
> In women's waxen hearts to set their forms!
> Alas, our frailty is the cause, not we!
> For such as we are made of, such we be.
> How will this fadge? my master loves her dearly;

And I, poor monster, fond as much on him;
And she, mistaken, seems to dote on me.
What will become of this? As I am man,
My state is desperate for my master's love;
As I am woman,— now alas the day!—
What thriftless sighs shall poor Olivia breathe!
O time! thou must untangle this, not I;
It is too hard a knot for me to untie!

Now let's have a look at some possible interpolations.

> VIOLA: *(What the hell?)* I left no ring with her: what means this lady?
> *(OMFG!)* Fortune forbid my outside have not charm'd her!
> *(Let's examine this.)* She made good view of me; indeed, so much,
> That sure methought her eyes had lost her tongue,
> For she did speak in starts distractedly.
> *(I think I'm right!)* She loves me, sure; *(And here's another bit of evidence)* the cunning of her passion
> Invites me in this churlish messenger.
> *(Malvolio's talking rubbish!)* None of my lord's ring! *(And here's the reason.)* why, he sent her none.
> *(Yes, I'm positive.)* I am the man: *(Oh dear, let's think about this.)* if it be so, as 'tis,
> Poor lady, she were better love a dream.
> *(I've done a bad, bad thing.)* Disguise, I see, thou art a wickedness,
> Wherein the pregnant enemy does much.
> *(Why are we women so weak?)* How easy is it for the proper-false
> In women's waxen hearts to set their forms!
> *(Oh well, can't be helped.)* Alas, our frailty is the cause, not we!
> For such as we are made of, such we be.
> How will this fadge? *(Right, let's analyse this.)* My master loves her dearly;

And I, poor monster, fond as much on him;
And she, mistaken, seems to dote on me.
(So, what's going to happen?) What will become of this?
(It's not looking good, is it?) As I am man,
My state is desperate for my master's love;
As I am woman, *(And there's another complication.)* — now alas the day! —
What thriftless sighs shall poor Olivia breathe!
(I give up.) O time! thou must untangle this, not I;
It is too hard a knot for me to untie!

These are by no means the only possibilities. Some of those brackets could emphasise the humour of the situation – it is a comedy after all. But as a device to help refine intention and to get away from the piece just sounding like a block of amorphous words, brackets are really helpful. And if I'm being honest I'd say I use a wordless form of brackets every time I act.

Teaching Comedy

As I slowly started to get a handle on this coaching business, I kept getting asked by drama schools to teach comedy. This was a whole new kettle of fish. For a start, I had to work out what I thought 'comedy acting' was and how to impart those thoughts.

I always began by explaining what I'd discovered with Matt Cameron's radio sketch and then rediscovered as the innkeeper in the film *Take Away*. That there is no difference between 'comedy acting' and 'dramatic acting'. And I repeated it. And reinforced it. I was quite definite.

'There is no difference between comic and dramatic acting.'

But there is of course. As the students pointed out.

There's timing and delivery. What I call the externalities. These things are crucial in comedy. If you pause too long or don't pause long enough between the feedline and the punchline, you won't get your laugh. If you stress the wrong word, you won't get your laugh. If you don't articulate the line properly, you won't get your laugh. (And if you've ever told a funny story or a joke and then stumbled over the punchline, you'll have experienced this last one. The laugh's not there.) The line has to come out perfectly or the moment's ruined. Which is why comedy is so much more difficult than straight drama. Because beyond all the rigmarole of the acting process, which is the same for both forms, the shape of the performance, or the form, has to be *just right* for comedy. There's a whole other layer of complexity.

The best way to work out the right timing for a line, or the best way to deliver a comic moment, is just air miles. Like anything. Doing it and doing it and doing it. And watching other actors. But there's two ways of looking at it which have always helped me: the Popped Balloon and the Blank Sheet of Paper.

Don't pop the balloon too soon. If the lines before the laugh are the balloon being inflated, then the punchline is the popping of the balloon.

I bought a thesaurus yesterday. When I got home, I discovered the pages were blank. I have no words to describe my disappointment.

It's not the funniest joke in the world but it'll do for our purposes. Like any joke there's a ratcheting up of tension, we're waiting for the pay-off, the suspense mounts and then there's a sudden release, the balloon pops and we laugh. But if you pop the balloon too soon, if you release the tension before it's ready to be released, the laugh will disappear. If I was on stage telling this joke and someone in the audience stood and shouted, 'That's a pity. You'd better take it back!' just before the punchline, then the balloon would pop too early, the tension would be gone and I'd never get my laugh.

> ME: I bought a thesaurus yesterday. When I got home I discovered the pages were blank.
> SOMEONE ELSE: That's a pity. You'd better take it back!
> ME: [*feebly*] I have no words to describe my disappointment.
>
> *Silence and tumbleweeds. We hear a frog croak.*

Often the early popping of the balloon is actually laughter itself. When we film *Mad as Hell* we get a studio audience in to provide laughter. This audience is obviously composed of those who like the show so much that they want to come and see it put together. They're fans. On top of that they are worked up to such a fever of hilarity by the warm-up guy that it really doesn't take much to set them off. Many times, they have found the feed-line of a gag to be funny enough to laugh at. And having laughed at the feed-line, they physically can't laugh at the laugh line. It's too soon. They need another line or two in between, lines that aren't laughed at. That set up the next joke. And only then are they ready to laugh again. You can't get a laugh at the feed-line *and* the pay-off.

Sometimes actors deliberately pop the balloon too soon by adding something funny before the pay-off, but often it's at the expense of the moment and of the whole momentum of the play. They get a laugh but it's the wrong one.

Years after my disgraceful counting of the audience in *Accidental Death of an Anarchist* I was asked to do an adaptation of the play for the Sydney Theatre Company. This time for an all female cast. I wasn't present at rehearsals – I think it's often better for the writer to disappear during that time – so the director and the actors can make the play theirs.

Consequently, I saw the play for the first time at the first preview. One of the highlights was the actor playing Inspector Pisani – it was a brilliant performance, funny, scary and delightful. I did have one tiny issue though.

In the second act, the Maniac suggests Pisani has been beating up the suspect. Pisani denies this and claims they were just having a bit of a laugh. The next exchange goes like this.

> MADMAN: I see they've changed the police motto. How does it go again?
> INSPECTOR: 'Helping the citizens of Italy.'
> MADMAN: Yes, now it's 'Helping the citizens of Italy soil their undergarments with laughter.'

Not a big laugh, but a reasonably faithful version of the original Italian.

When I came to see it, the actor had added to their line. It became

> MADMAN: I see they've changed the police motto. How does it go again?
> INSPECTOR: 'Helping the citizens of Italy……NOT!'
> MADMAN: Yes, now it's 'Helping the citizens of Italy soil their undergarments with laughter.'

She got a huge laugh, bigger than the original, but it was the wrong laugh. She had popped the balloon too soon and the real punchline never worked.

So what, you may say, a laugh is a laugh, how can it be wrong? And if it's a bigger laugh, then surely that's better. And you'd have a point. But when the laugh died down and the Madman said her line, which should have been the laugh-line, and which sounded like a laugh-line, there was an awkward silence. The audience had already had their laugh, before the punchline. The tension had been punctured, the balloon had been popped and they weren't going to laugh again. Not until the next joke was built up. But it was clear to all that a line that should have got a laugh didn't, a false note had been struck, the Madman seemed lessened somehow, the momentum of the lines disappeared and something seemed not quite right.

Moreover, the relationship between the two was subtly contradicted. Up till then, the Inspector had been denying any suggestion of police wrongdoing. This moment seemed to undermine that completely.

A big laugh had been created but at a cost. To the energy of the play and to its truth. And one of the immutable laws of comedy had been broken – don't put a joke on another joke.

So the question is, what are you sacrificing for this laugh? And is the price too high?

The Blank Sheet of Paper is another way of viewing the issue. You're trying to create a moment. Of laughter. ***And the moment will be more effective if it's not competing with anything else. If it is drawn on a blank sheet of paper.*** If the paper is torn or creased or scribbled on, then the effect will be less. The moment won't stand out among all the mess and you won't get your laugh. It may be that putting your hands in your pockets, or scratching your chin, is messing up that blank sheet of paper. Perhaps try stillness, instead. It may be that action behind you is messing up the paper. Again, stillness might help. If nothing else is happening during the line, then it has a greater chance of the audience focusing in on it. Those shuffly feet of mine in *The Club* are a perfect example of the not-blank sheet of paper. How can you expect people to focus on what you're saying, and laugh, if you're distracting them, even slightly, with your twitchy feet?

But there's still more to comedy. Yes, don't forget to act and commit and be truthful. And yes, your timing matters. But all this is skirting around the issue of what that indefinable difference actually is between comic and serious acting – and I think it's something to do with the level of commitment. ***You need to commit, certainly, but perhaps not too much.***

I once ran a workshop on comedy with a group of students. One of them was working on a scene from Tom Stoppard's *Rosencrantz and Guildenstern are Dead*. He was somehow killing the laughter every time they ran it. It wasn't anything to do with commitment or truth, he always tried and he always gave a hundred and fifty per cent. I sighed and put it down to my deficiencies as a teacher, or (more likely) the boy just didn't have what it takes. I turned my attention to the others.

I gave two of them a scene from the film *Garage Days*. A girl breaks up with her boyfriend when she discovers he's slept with someone else. We worked on it and it turned out to be quite an amusing scene. She breaks up with him, he sits dejectedly on the sofa and gets her quick unpick (a sharp needle-like tool for unpicking stitches) stuck in his bum and she has to pull it out.

The next day I had to work elsewhere and they rehearsed it with another teacher. When I got back, they ran it for me. All the comedy had gone out of the scene. I couldn't work it out. The blocking was the same, the lines were the same but the comedy had gone. I asked them what the teacher had said the day before.

'He told me to play it as if I was still in love with him', the girl said.

And that was the key. Watching the scene, I was feeling too sorry for the girl to laugh. It became a sad scene. And I realised that, in comedy, perhaps we don't always want the audience to engage too much. If you empathise too deeply with the character, you don't have that distance that enables you to laugh at their plight.

It's a fine line we're dealing with here, of course. Yes, audiences need to engage, but lightly enough to be able to laugh at what happens. If we empathise too much, then the laughter goes. So we need to commit to the truth of the situation, but *not too much*.

There's no such limitation with more serious stuff, of course. A few months later, I went to see this same group of students do a version of the Ancient Greek myth, *Electra*. Passion and hatred and killing your mother and being in love with your sister. And not a giggle anywhere.

And my student, who I had decided was not up to it, was a revelation. His ability to commit to violent extremes of emotion suited the demands of the play perfectly – it had been just too strong a brew for the Stoppard. On the other hand, some of my students who had seemed to have a real feel for comedy were completely out of their depth.

Comedy is stifled if we over-commit and superficial if we don't commit enough.

A gross generalisation, but there's something in it, I think.

It's one of the reasons that film and comedy don't really mix. I know this will not be a popular view, but the truly great films, the ones that make the top ten films of all time lists, are never comedies. Film does drama so much better.

The great filmic device is the close-up, a device which takes you right into the character's thoughts and feelings. You can't laugh at someone whose emotions you're being overwhelmed with. You're too close to them.

That's not to say that all film comedies are rubbish – quite patently that's not true. But comedy is not what film does best. Cinema's power is to engulf us. And that inhibits laughter.

But we mustn't forget, while we struggle to pinpoint exactly what it is that makes a performance comic, that perhaps we shouldn't go too far in the wrong direction.

I had given a group of students some comic scenes – Oscar Wilde, Tom Stoppard et cetera – and I was watching a couple of them go through their paces. They were struggling with the scene and I just couldn't find the words to help them.

At last in desperation and just to give them something to do, I asked them to do it much more quickly. I was a little ashamed of myself. Surely there was something internal I could find to help them? Apparently not. Just do it quicker.

But the result was amazing. Not only was the scene a pleasure to watch now, as it had life and energy, but they were hitting all of the notes I'd given them about specific moments, which they hadn't been able to achieve before. They'd been trying too hard and it was destroying the lightness of the comedy.

Sometimes all you need to do is lighten up and speed up. There's a real tendency among young actors to pause and slow down.

And it really doesn't help comedy. Don't try so hard here. Float. Glide. Run.

Of course speeding up is not necessarily about speaking faster, it's about energy and less pausing. And jumping on your cues. But sometimes speaking faster is exactly what it's about.

Morecambe and Wise were a much loved British comedy duo. They had a TV show in Britain in the 70s. They often had guests on, to help them with their sketches. Actress Glenda Jackson, not known for comedy, was one such. The story goes that as she was getting ready to make her entrance, she had a sudden panicked thought. She turned to the two of them.

'What's my motivation?'

'Fast and loud', was the immediate response.

It's not a silly reply. You can't hang around with comedy. And you can't hang back either. If in doubt, raise the volume and increase speed.

And I have to say, slowness is not really your friend in more serious stuff either. So often, our striving for significance or high stakes pushes us into long pauses.

> To be [*pause*] or not to be, [*longer pause*] that is the question.
> Quite lengthy pause.
> Whether 'tis [*another pause*] nobler [*and another*] in the mind
> [*really quite excruciatingly long pause*] to suffer –

Et cetera, et cetera. You get the point.

But you only pause for a reason. If you're just stopping for effect you're doing it wrong. Why have you stopped? What's going through your head? Or your heart? And if it's nothing, then don't pause. The only argument I can see for that first pause is that you're searching for the words, but presumably you know what the question is before you speak so you know what the words are. Presumably also you want to express this idle thought, so why are you dawdling? If you've forgotten the lines, then you have to stop, or if a Boeing 747 flies overhead or someone has a heart attack in the audience then I can see an argument for waiting, but if not, get on with it. If the pause isn't meaningful, then the audience will know, and get restless.

And anyway, you have to earn your pauses. Even in serious drama there's a rhythm to attend to. Don't pause. Don't pause. Don't pause. And now you've earned your pause. So use it.

Comedy. A mysterious business. I still haven't got a handle on it. I do know that I can take the comedy out of a scene or a line, or put it in, just by changing gears somehow, but I'm not sure just exactly how I do it. So there's some difference in technique. I also know that just when I think I've got the whole thing nailed, something happens to make me have to rethink the whole thing. It's an ongoing process of working it out and it's not finished for me by a long shot.

My Mantra

It's not really mine. I read it in a book, by Terence Crawford. Whom I've mentioned before.

Words are just the noise the scene makes.

This is a brilliant way of looking at the whole thing. It's the sentence I say to students the most. More often than 'Quiet' or 'Someone has to go first'. Or 'No, we can't play a game'. I think it sums up the whole thing perfectly.

In Act II Scene i of *A Midsummer Night's Dream* Hermione pursues Demetrius into the forest. He is in love with Hermia and Hermione's in love with him. A desperate man frantically looks for the girl he's obsessed with, maddened by the fact that she's gone off with someone else. He's infuriated further by being followed everywhere he goes by his ex. She is, in turn, so obsessed by him and so desperate for his approval that she has helped him in his quest for her rival. That's how low she's sunk.

There's a lot of wild emotion and conflicting desire washing about here. They both frantically want something they just can't get. That's what the scene's about. Of course the words are important, they express what the characters are feeling. But they are only important in that they are the expression of what's going on inside. And unless you start from the emotions and the wishes and desires of these two, you don't have a scene. But what a scene, if you do.

It's the secret to doing monologues well. What state is the character in before they start speaking? In a sense, the performance of the monologue needs to start in the moment before the character opens their mouth, because ***if you don't enter in the right emotional state, all you have is words.*** But if you do, then the words just ride out of you, carried by the emotions and intentions of the scene. They are just the noise that the scene makes. Brilliant.

three things

Whenever I teach nowadays, I sit the students down at the end of the last day and I look at them significantly and I tell them this.

There are three ways you can become a better actor.

1. *Learn.* Keep on doing what you're doing. Go to drama school, go to classes, practise at home, do scenes with your friends. It's a craft and it needs to be learnt. It's a muscle and it needs to be exercised. So learn and then practise. And keep learning.
2. *Live.* This is a profession where, all other things being equal, you become a better actor the longer you live. The more stuff you go through, the more different situations you find yourself in, the bigger your emotional library and the more nuanced and subtle your work becomes. 'I recognise this situation. I know what it feels like.' The work is done for you. You've been on that football field and you've whacked heads with someone and you don't have to imagine it anymore, because you've done it.

And

3. *Read.* Experience as much as you can of whatever humans have created on the subject of the human condition. Which is everything. Read, go to the theatre, listen to music, of all kinds, go to the art gallery, go to the cinema. Absorb.

These things benefit you in ways you're often not even aware of, and certainly would not expect. I once worked out how to solve the problems of Shakespeare's problematic *Troilus and Cressida* at an Impressionist exhibition at the National Gallery. By accident. I wasn't intending to mount a production of the play and I haven't since, but if the opportunity comes up, I'm ready.

Most important, however, is to read. Read novels and plays and poetry. Read everything.

I can't stress this enough. Reading gives you so, so much.

The more you read, the more new ideas you absorb, and the more new situations you experience.

The more you read, the more you are able to comprehend the structure of a play or a script, and the more you understand the style of the work, where it stands in relation to other work and what is possible within it and what isn't.

The more you read, the better your script analysis becomes.

The more you read, the greater your powers of concentration.

What's even more beautiful about reading is that it puts you into the head of someone else. It forces you to abandon your view of the world and take on another's. In other words, **reading gives you empathy.**

Read a book and you become a better actor.

And this third way is just as important as the other two. And it's never too late to start.

Read a book and you'll become a better actor.

But Snapchat and glossy magazines and online games – they don't give you anything.

'Please', I say to them, 'whatever you do from here on in, find a book and read it.'

And then I say goodbye and good luck and leave.

Goodbye. And good luck.

Acknowledgements

This book came into being because of two men: James Laurie, who urged me to write something; and the late, great and much lamented John Clarke, whose conversation about the importance of structure helped me to find the form of what you have just read. I am indebted to them both.

Thanks to my wife Louise for her wise advice, and for helping formulate the title of this book, and to my brother William for his valuable input.

Shelley Lush from the State Theatre Company (SA), Judith Seeff from Sydney Theatre Company, Georgia Fox from Melbourne Theatre Company and Caraline Douglas of Malthouse Theatre Company were all extremely helpful in finding photographs. As was Anna Tregloan. I am grateful for their help.

Thanks to Shaun Micallef for permission to use some of his work.

And to Jeff Busby, Lisa Tomasetti, David Wilson, Eric Algra, Tracey Schramm, Jodie Hutchinson and Nikki Hamilton-Cornwall for permission to use theirs.

And lastly thanks to Currency Press for taking a punt on an unrealised idea, and Claire Grady especially for her support, advice and the astuteness of her editing.

Bibliography

Barkworth, P. (1980) *About Acting*. London: Martin Secker &Warburg Limited

Crawford, T. (2012) *Dimensions of Acting: An Australian Approach*. Sydney: Currency Press

Donnellan, D. (2002) *The Actor and the Target*. London and New York: Theatre Communications Group & Nick Hern Books

Fine, H. (2014) *Fine On Acting: A Vision of the Craft*. Los Angeles: Havenhurst Books

Johnstone, K. (1985) *Impro: Improvisation and the Theatre*. London: Methuen

Moss, L. (2005) *The Intent to Live: Achieving your true potential as an Actor*. New York: Bantam Dell

Francis Greenslade is a familiar face to TV and theatre audiences, having been a freelance actor for over thirty years. He is a regular on the ABC's satirical comedy, *Shaun Micallef's Mad As Hell* and spent five years as Brian Gross, the father of Jenny Gross, in Channel 7's family drama *Winners and Losers*.

His other TV credits include *The Leftovers, The Micallef Programme, Jack Irish, Doctor Blake, Full Frontal, Blue Heelers, It's a Date, Offspring, Bed of Roses, It's a Date* and *City Homicide*.

He is also a prolific theatre actor. His theatre credits include Melbourne Theatre Company's *Shakespeare in Love, The Odd Couple, 33 Variations, The Club, School for Scandal, Funerals and Circuses* and *Urinetown*. He has worked with most of the theatre companies in Australia.

Francis is also a writer. He was commissioned to translate and adapt Feydeau's *The Girl from Maxim* and his adaptation of *Accidental Death of an Anarchist* was produced by Sydney Theatre Company in 2018.

www.ingramcontent.com/pod-product-compliance
Lightning Source LLC
Chambersburg PA
CBHW040306170426
43194CB00022B/2917